Unlikely Teachers

JUDY RINGER

Unlikely Teachers

FINDING THE
HIDDEN GIFTS IN
DAILY CONFLICT

Foreword by Thomas Crum

To Sharon ~
With Ki!
Judy Ringer

ONEPOINT PRESS
PORTSMOUTH, NH

Printed in the United States of America

ISBN-13: 978-0-9776149-0-5
ISBN-10: 0-9776149-0-5
Library of Congress Control Number: 2006900547

Book and cover design by Lisa Scontras Noonis
Managing Editor, Sonja Hakala

Portions of this book previously appeared in *Aikido Today Magazine*. The author wishes to thank the editors and readers of *Aikido Today Magazine* for their support.

Inquiries and orders should be addressed to:
OnePoint Press
76 Park Street
Portsmouth, NH 03801

This book is dedicated to my teachers,
the ones I know and the ones I have yet to meet.
Thank you very much.

*Centering is the art
of being fully alive.
And wherever the
art of centering
is practiced,
things change
dramatically.*

– Thomas Crum

Contents

Part Five: *Power*

Part Six: *Teachers*

Foreword

Do you have a passion? Something that, when you do it, you forget about time and all your worries and even lunch? If there are fifty workshop participants in the room when I ask this question, I may get fifty distinct answers—from "working on a motorcycle" to "ballroom dancing." But what do they all have in common? It is simply this: when engaged in that activity, each workshop participant is aware and connected.

When you are fully aware and deeply connected, time stops. You are in fascination and completely present, whether you are painting the ceiling of the Sistine Chapel or standing along the river, casting with a fly rod. Solo, maybe, but never alone, because there is a flowing river of connection that dissolves the separation between you and the world around you. No wonder hours, fatigue, even the need to eat come and go. Your heart and your playful spirit are fully engaged.

Couldn't we all use more of this on our own paths? In this wonderful book, Judy guides us to creating greater connection and awareness on our journeys. Her stories help us consider our own stories and the gifts of learning that they have been to us. The principles in this book will help us proceed along the path with utmost sincerity and a sense of discovery, creating magic and awakening along the way. And we'll find lots of growing pains, too, because with every worthy journey we must be open to the peeling away of our many layers of resistance—the physical tension, the mental frustration, the emotional upheaval—until our heart is wide open.

Judy shows us that the best of lessons occur when we least expect them. It behooves us to live a life of possibility rather than expectation. What if the biggest joke of all is that everyone we meet is the Christ or the Buddha in disguise? What if every situation—waiting in a long line, getting a rejection slip, suffering a broken heart—introduces us to a master teacher, providing us with an opportunity to become more patient, a better listener, more self aware, more compassionate? Unlikely teachers indeed!

I've known Judy for more than twenty years, both as my student and as an esteemed colleague. She artfully articulates important concepts in this book, it is true. But what is more essential—she lives and breathes them every day in her own life. The tears and laughter of a worthy practice have peeled away her layers powerfully and gracefully. You can read this between the lines: Judy Ringer's heart is wide open.

Enjoy, savor, and learn as you read *Unlikely Teachers,* and remember one thing: your teacher is right in front of you, maybe in your very next breath.

Thomas Crum, Author
The Magic of Conflict
Journey to Center
Three Deep Breaths

Preface

*If you don't like
what's happening in your life,
change your mind.*

– The Dalai Lama

On This Planet

My husband Jim and I had planned a special dinner out. Our
birthdays are just two weeks apart, and we usually celebrate
them together. We wanted the evening to be memorable, so I
made reservations at a restaurant we'd never visited but that
had a reputation for exceptional food and elegant ambience.

The big night arrived. The evening was cold (we were born
in January), but we were warm, convivial, looking good, and
anticipating a new experience.

The hostess met us at the door, took our coats, and ushered
us into the warm, candlelit dining room. She showed us to a
lovely table for two and pulled out our chairs. It was perfect.
But as I sat down, my ears were assaulted by the piercing cry
of a baby at the table directly across the aisle. I turned and saw
a party of five—the baby, two parents, and two others. Mom
tried tending to the crying infant, and the others looked
embarrassed. My mood plummeted. I like children, especially
babies, but not crying at the top of their lungs in a café de
haute cuisine. I did not want to spend my evening and a pile
of money being entertained by the wails of a howling infant.

I saw the birthday celebration in ruins, the serenity of a quiet, romantic evening drowned out by the din at the next table. I was beside myself—uncentered, judgmental, angry. I could not fathom how anyone could bring an infant to a place like this. What were they thinking? Had they no conception of dining etiquette? In my world, babies stay home when their parents go out for an elegant dinner. That's why we have babysitters.

The waitress came by and asked if we wanted a cocktail. We said we'd hold off a moment, we wanted to examine the menu. Jim and I stared at each other. Should we stay or go? We had been eagerly anticipating our date, the menu looked great, and we wanted to enjoy the wonderful evening we'd planned. But how could that happen in this suddenly changed atmosphere?

We talked about what to do. We knew if we stayed, we would have to make peace somehow with our surroundings. But was that possible? And if we left, we faced the inconvenience of finding a new place to eat, in the cold, without reservations. Our night out was heading downhill fast.

The baby quieted a little. The sharp screaming moderated to an unhappy whine. The waitress returned. Keeping our options open, we ordered a cocktail but no food. I was still thinking what a nightmare this was when Jim leaned over and quietly suggested we play a little game of "Let's Pretend." Let's pretend we live on a planet, he said, where babies are honored, even revered, and considered extremely lucky. They are incredibly powerful beings and to be seated near one in a public place, especially on a big night out, is seen as a sign of immense good fortune. We were favored, chosen by fate to be seated within a few feet of this amazing being.

On this planet we had the best table in the house, the envy of all.

And just like that we were suddenly on another planet and my attitude was transformed. I believed it, and it was true. The most extraordinary part of the transformation was that it took no time. I was on one planet, then I was on another, and it was a remarkable place—delightful, carefree, lovely. Why wouldn't I want to live here? It was so much more pleasant. I was so much more pleasant. It was as if I were the child, playing, discovering, fascinated with everything and everyone. Just like that we became the luckiest people in the room. We had been singled out for a year in which all our birthday wishes would come true.

We ordered dinner, soaking up the presence of the small creature across the way. We smiled at the child but were careful not to look over too often. Of course, on this planet the family was aware of the good omen they carried with them. Still, not wanting to make them uncomfortable, we would sneak a peak only now and then to marvel at our luckiness.

Appetizers arrived, and they were, of course, delicious. The baby settled down, making playful sounds and cooing with its mother. Entrées were graciously laid before us— wonderful. Dessert—enchanting. The evening was blissful, much better than anything we could have imagined. We were sad when the family left before we did, but we knew we had been painted with their baby's brush of happiness.

We wandered home, still delighting in the atmosphere of the Lucky Baby Planet and our remarkable good fortune in discovering it. Not surprisingly, we've had subsequent opportunities for more planetary adventures. Since then, we've visited the planet of the Lucky Traffic Jam, and the one where the 5 a.m. crow concert is about the best thing that could ever happen. Each time we find ourselves in the presence of young children in a public place, Jim and I remember to visit our Lucky Baby Planet and transform our surroundings.

The game of "Let's Pretend" is a game we probably all played as children. I think we continue to play as adults—we just forget we're playing. Whenever we use our imagination to turn a seemingly negative event into a positive one, we're playing. Sometimes we do the opposite and turn what could be a lovely experience into a nightmare. That magical night, Jim and I simply decided to pretend on purpose and our world changed for the better. The stories that follow are about practicing this game more often and learning to play it at will.

What planet are you on? If something is bothering you, can you pretend that the irritation is a gift? What if it really is? The more I look for opportunities to enlarge my understanding of conflict, the more hidden gifts I find.

Unlikely Teachers

Harmony doesn't mean getting along with people at any cost just to avoid a confrontation. Harmony as used in aikido does not involve compromising at all. Rather aikido's harmony brings different, even opposing, elements together and intensifies them in a way that drives everything toward a higher level.

— Mitsunari Kanai, *Technical Aikido*

Introduction

Always practice the Art of Peace
in a vibrant and joyful manner.

– Morihei Ueshiba, *O Sensei*, Founder of Aikido

Hidden Gifts

Conflict stories are our most interesting stories. When you see
two people deeply engaged in conversation, chances are one
of them is telling a conflict story. They're fascinating. And we
have such strong opinions about them, especially when they
are *our* stories. We live them again and again as we revisit
the events, the feelings, the thoughts about what we should
have said, and how perfect things could be if only our
adversaries would change.

The moment of conflict holds such promise: the
opportunity to approach life creatively, make a different
choice, visit another planet—opportunities we would not
otherwise be offered if it weren't for the conflict. Conflict
is one way in which we come to know the world and
understand each other. Conflict offers an opening to our most
powerful selves. It also offers the opposite. Like two roads
diverging, one leads toward connection, the other toward
separation. Our habitual patterns of reaction leave us thinking
we have no choice but to do what we've always done. Then,
when the conflict is over, we look back, asking *Why did I do
that? What was I thinking?* having once again missed the
opportunity to take a different path.

Making Choices

Conflict too often provides the bricks and mortar for walls that keep out the world and those we love. Constructed of fear, judgment, defensiveness, and misunderstanding, our walls are meant to keep us safe and maintain the rightness of our opinions. The problem is that walls work two ways. Our carefully assembled grudges, justifications, and attitudes are, at the same time, barriers to what we desire most— connection to our wisdom, to our humanity, and to the source of universal intelligence that supports us all. Our real safety lies in connection, but because we are more practiced at building walls, we create a prison for ourselves, keeping out the very things we hoped the walls would enclose.

What walls have you constructed that no longer serve a useful purpose? Do reactive habits keep you from finding a new path? In what ways are you resisting connection? What is conflict and how can you safely change yourself in order to change your situation?

A New Way to Manage Conflict

Luckily, I've discovered a tool to help me remember I have alternatives even in the most difficult situations. A couple of decades ago, I fell in love with a martial art called aikido and began to see the world through its lens. From the beginning, aikido's fluid, spiraling, and powerful movements seemed to suggest possibility—a new way to manage physical conflict. I found aikido's principles of centered response, utilization of energy, and non-resistant leading to be equally applicable in non-physical conflict—what we might call life's "attacks"— such as arguments, everyday hassles, and the more serious problems we all face at some point in our lives.

When you watch aikidoists practicing, you don't see a typical adversarial battle between aggressor and defender. You see what looks like a physical exchange between two people giving and receiving energy, more like a powerful dance than combat.

As an attack comes toward her, the receiver does not strike back or otherwise block the force of the attack. Instead, she moves toward the incoming energy (shifting slightly off the line of attack) and physically unites with the attacker's power. Once she makes this connection, she controls the direction and momentum of the attack by pinning or throwing her opponent. This is the most basic principle of aikido: do not resist an attack. Instead, the aikidoist learns to blend, control, and redirect.

Utilization of Energy

Life could be a lot easier than I make it was my first thought upon seeing the art of aikido. Having lived the life of a perfectionist for so many years, I was accustomed to struggling with life events, putting pressure on myself at every turn. But as an aikidoist I asked, *How might I use what comes at me instead of fighting or wishing it away?* It made so much sense, and I loved the inclusive view it offered. I guessed correctly that it would take some undoing of old, ingrained habits of resistance before I could acquire this new way of being, and I began to look with new eyes at what I had previously thought of as negative events in my life. *What does it mean to use energy?*

I began to teach the aikido metaphor as a way of transforming conflict and to share the view the aikido lens offers, both to demonstrate for others and to clarify for myself how life, work, and relationships might benefit from this model. At the same time, I began practicing the martial art, reasoning that integrating aikido "on the mat" would help me teach and apply its concepts "off the mat." Every moment on the mat reinforces my belief.

The Way of Harmony

Developed in the twentieth century, aikido is the invention of a highly skilled and spiritual Japanese warrior, Morihei Ueshiba (1883–1969). Those of us who practice aikido call him *O Sensei* ("Great Teacher"). A master of sword and open-hand combat, *O Sensei* held that the true martial art was one of harmony. Making subtle changes in the combative arts he had mastered, he conceived a martial art that could disarm an attack without doing harm in the process. He called it aikido— the art of peace. Translated as "the way of blending or harmonizing with universal energy," the aim of aikido is not merely self-defense but a new way to reconcile differences.

The power and art of aikido are in the joining—in moving toward an attack and becoming one with the attacker. It takes presence of mind and a strong center of gravity not to be swept up in the energy of an attack but instead to enter into its chaos, understand its core, and direct it toward resolution. Since she flows *with* the river instead of pushing *against* it, the aikidoist's movements are quick and powerful. Before an attack can do harm, the attacker is engaged and guided to a place where the energy can play out safely.

In life, the aikido metaphor is realized when you transform challenges into opportunities and adapt to new circumstances with ease, moving *with* life's flow, instead of struggling *against* it. You are practicing aikido whenever you listen with curiosity to an opposing view or search for mutual understanding, respect, and purpose. Aikido happens any time you stop, take a breath, and choose a more felicitous state of being. No matter how you approach it, whether physically or conceptually, aikido offers a unique blend of power and grace.

Aikido and Conflict—The Metaphor

The stories that follow depict personal experiences, how I responded at the time, and what I learned. They also act as meditations on the aikido-conflict metaphor as it has evolved and crystallized for me. Each story falls into one of six facets of the metaphor as I imagine it playing out in the successful resolution of a conflict. Interrelated and inseparable from each other, the facets correlate with the way I have watched myself encounter, manage, and (most of the time) resolve conflict. The six facets are:

- **Resistance.** My initial reaction to adversity is to resist it. In a physical assault, I want to keep the attacker away from me. Similarly, I would rather not have to deal with a workplace conflict, a difficult person, or a frightening illness.

- **Connection.** At some point, however, I must connect with the conflict if there is any hope of resolving it. In aikido, I connect by moving toward the attacker and joining my energy with his. In life, I connect when I accept that the problem exists. Connection is the first step toward resolution.

- **Practice.** As I acknowledge the conflict, I begin to take action. At first my action is unskilled. I make mistakes, and I practice and refine my approach. Aikido practitioners refer to this refinement process as "getting on the mat." The mat is the place where we meet to learn and hone our technique and practice confidence and presence.

- **Discovery.** Through steady practice, I gradually find myself in new territory, where the realization of how little I know catapults me into a land of discovery. Whether on the aikido mat or on the mat of life, I become a learner. As I move from resistance to curiosity and wonder, my practice becomes fun.

- **Power.** Discovery brings a new kind of power because it is aligned with energy. I learn that power does not equal force or coercion. Rather, this new power increases in direct relationship to flexibility and empathy.

- **Teachers.** Finally, I notice that conflict has become my teacher. My difficult relationships have taught me flexibility and assertiveness. Through adversity, I have discovered new perspectives and insights. In aikido we say, "The attack is a gift of energy." I bow with gratitude.

Centered Response

Underlying and connecting the six facets of the aikido-conflict metaphor is my ability to direct my life energy in a conscious and purposeful way. Call it what you will—self-control, emotion management—my awareness of and ability to manage *me* is where each story begins. On the aikido mat, when the attack comes, we learn to "center and extend *ki.*"

To be "centered" in this sense means to be balanced, calm, and connected to an inner source of power. In life as in aikido, when you're centered, you are more effective, capable, and in control. As the book unfolds, you will learn how to choose the centered state when conflict arises.

Ki (pronounced "key") is Japanese for energy or universal life force. It is the *ch'i* in *tai ch'i* or *qi* in *qi gong*. When you center and extend *ki,* you increase your ability to influence your environment and your relationships.

Bowing In

At each aikido practice, we bow to each other as we get onto the mat to begin our learning—as I now bow to you. Thank you for picking up these stories on how to be more purposeful in inventing your life, day by day and moment by moment.

Like you, I am a learner and an explorer, and much of what I write is influenced by curiosity, not certainty. When I first started using the aikido metaphor, I thought I was using it to teach about conflict. Now I know that my interest in conflict is actually a fascination with how I interact with people and events in my life, and with how I give and receive energy and co-create meaning with other human beings.

The people and events in these stories have proven to be gifts in my life, though they did not always appear that way at first. My hope is to share the insights and new skills that came as a result of these interactions. I will be happy if a story becomes a reminder to take a moment and regain perspective, perhaps at the beginning or the end of the day, or in the middle of a difficult challenge. I hope that these stories may act as a breath of fresh air and cause you to remember your own experiences and the gifts that came with them.

Each story ends with a Practice—questions and exercises to help you work with the concepts and increase your power, your presence, and your enjoyment of life. Many stories also include comments from students, friends, and colleagues who have their own conflict stories to tell.

I often say to workshop participants that I have nothing new to teach. I think we know how we want to be, but it is often difficult to act on that knowing. You'll see this is true for me. I'm still practicing.

Many other wonderful books have been written on these topics, and at the end of this book, I've included a list of resources you may find helpful on your journey.

1

Resistance

When the attack comes,

my first reaction is to try and stop it.

I don't want this in my life.

I didn't ask for it,

and I don't want it.

But it pushes back.

It wants in.

Life is asking us to use
the energy and spirit of
people and problems
we feel are against us.
All we have to do is
change or reverse our
ideas of who we are.

– Arnold Mindell, *The Leader as Martial Artist*

Choosing My Self

All things change when we do.

– Kukei, Eighth-Century Zen Master

I keep two little pieces of paper taped to the telephone in my office. One says "Center," the other "Breathe." These two reminders were facing me the day I picked up the handset to call the customer service department of a nationally recognized banking institution. My mother has a loan with the bank and had tried to get their service department to send me duplicate statements every month. For many reasons, she likes me to know what's going on in her financial life, and I receive statements from a variety of companies on her behalf. Mom told me she had called the bank twice with no success. I decided to take matters into my own hands.

After some time and confusion over my request, Eva, the customer service representative, said I would need to send them a power of attorney for my mother along with a written request. Then they would send the monthly statement to me instead of sending it to my mother. I said, no, I wanted a duplicate. I wanted us both to get a statement. She said that was impossible.

Pushing Buttons
It's an understatement to say that customer service is one of those subjects that can trigger uncentered behavior in me. If I

think that I'm being treated poorly or that the company should be able to accommodate me and won't, I can lose my temper very quickly. This was one of those times. I was flabbergasted. I could not comprehend that an institution of such quality and size could not handle this simple request.

I told Eva how amazed I was since, in my view, I was asking for such a small service. It was ridiculous that they could not manage what others handle easily enough. I could tell I was getting nowhere, except increasingly frustrated. I also sensed that Eva was becoming resistant on the other end of the phone line. If I kept pushing, one of us would eventually hang up and both of us would stew in our own juices—for who knows how long.

To injure an opponent is to injure yourself.
To control aggression without inflicting injury
is the Art of Peace.

– Morihei Ueshiba, *O Sensei,* Founder of Aikido

A Useful Question Is Worth a Thousand Words
I may have caught sight of my telephone reminders or maybe I just came to my senses—literally. I didn't like the way I felt—body, mind, or spirit. I took a deep breath to center myself and asked, "So what can we do?" And I was quiet. Eva said, "Well, I don't know, because data management says they can't send more than one statement a month. It's all on computer. I wish I could."

Whew—what a feeling. My whole body relaxed. I was now talking to a person. I also felt Eva relax, and I knew whatever happened next would be okay. I said, "You sound frustrated. I'm probably not the only person who's called with this kind of request." And, of course, I wasn't. As it turns out, she gets these calls daily and doesn't like being blamed for something she can't control. She'd love to oblige. But her pleas for help to data management always fall on deaf ears. I asked if there was anything I could do. She said writing a letter to the director of servicing might help, and I said I would. In the meantime, I asked if she could send a copy of this month's statement. "Of course, I'd be happy to do that," she said. We were friends now, helping each other out.

So I wrote the letter and copied Eva. I never heard back from the bank, but that's all right. My challenge was not what I thought it was that day. As I removed myself from winning the contest over a duplicate statement, I realized that the prize was not that important. I could live without it. Eventually the bank will straighten out its software problems, and in the meantime I know that when I need a statement, I can call Eva. We have a connection.

———•—•———

Aikido masters say that opposing an attack directly feeds it.
You may stop the other person temporarily,
but you don't stop his or her intention to attack.

— Andy Bryner and Dawna Markova, Ph.D., *An Unused Intelligence*

———•—•———

Listen and Learn

Resistance is not one-sided. It doesn't cause itself. It's a response to something—an idea, a request, a belief. For example, the more I pushed for my way, the more Eva pushed back. To reduce resistance, I let go of the need to get my point across, valid though it was from my perspective. As soon as Eva felt the pressure lessen, she could relax. Once she didn't have to push back against me, she could mentally and emotionally move to a new place. It's critical to understand that while she was engaged in fighting me, she couldn't actually change her position because she was busy protecting herself. But the minute I gave up my need to make her change, she had the freedom to do it on her own.

Is there a situation like this in your life? If there is, do you almost *feel* the resistance from the other person in a physical way? To alleviate the pressure, check out what's going on for the other person. Say something like "What can we do here?" or "Tell me how you see it." Wait and watch what happens. Her physiology and attitude will change, and you'll sense a lightening of the friction between you. Plus, if you're sincerely interested, you'll learn a lot. Truly listening requires you to drop your agenda momentarily. This isn't easy, but it's your key to transforming resistance into something more valuable.

In *The Dance of Connection,* author Harriet Lerner writes that in difficult conversations the task is not to "be yourself" but to "choose your self." There are many selves inside each of us. When we take action, we want to call on the self that speaks for the values we hold and the virtues we subscribe to, not the self that is reactively aggressive or acquiescent. Finding *that* self takes practice and intention. Difficult situations and challenging individuals become opportunities to choose with awareness.

People ask me what is needed in order to resolve the difficult issues facing this country and this planet. I think we need to resolve our own personal conflicts first, with loved ones, co-workers, and acquaintances, and within ourselves. The problems are not "out there" nor is the power to resolve them "out there." Both the problems and the power to resolve them reside in each and every one of us.

PRACTICE

Is there a person in your life whom you are resisting? Try easing the tension between you by asking him how he sees things or what he thinks the solution is to your disagreement. The problem may turn out to be a gift in disguise.

DREE'S STORY

I went to return a music book to a store where the proprietor had told me they don't accept returned music. I remembered your story about working with a customer service person who didn't want to help. You took the approach that you and the other person could work together and find an acceptable outcome for all parties. I knew that I wanted to buy a more expensive book and hoped the proprietor would go for an exchange. She did. And I didn't have to say anything. I think it was my mind-set (center? ki?) that spoke for me. And she had the new book in stock, so I returned the one I didn't want and got the one I wanted, all without a hitch. How good is that?

Singing Images of Fire

a hand moves and the fire's whirling takes
different shapes.
... all things change when we do.

the first word, ah,
blossomed into all others
each of them is true

you want to know about creativity
move your hand

all things change when we do

— Kukei, Eighth-Century Zen Master

Listening
When It's Not Easy

*Connected listening happens when
you are truly interested in understanding
the other person's feelings, interests, and
beliefs on a particular issue.*

– Thomas Crum, *The Magic of Conflict*

Once while teaching a course called "Conflict in the
Classroom" on how to manage problem students and
situations, a potential conflict arose for me in the first fifteen
minutes of the session.

A participant raised his hand and—with some passion—
asked how it was that I could use aikido, a Japanese martial
art with a philosophical foundation, as a metaphor in teaching
about conflict and communication. He said that if he, as a
practicing Christian, got up to speak about Christian values as
a basis for behavior, he would probably be shouted off the
stage. He had come to class to learn specific strategies to
manage conflict and handle difficult students, not to learn
about aikido or its philosophy. He said that if the class was
going to focus on aikido, he would leave.

There was silence. The class, as one, held its breath.
Fortunately, I did not.

I honestly replied that I did not know the answer to his
question about why it seemed culturally okay for me to use

aikido as a metaphor when he could not use Christianity in the same way, and I agreed with him that it didn't seem fair. I said I appreciated his viewpoint and his openness, and assured him that he had come to the right place. Aikido was a reference point we would use periodically, and at the end of the day he would leave with the mental and verbal strategies he was seeking to manage difficult situations, both in and out of the classroom.

Blending and Redirecting

This experience is interesting to me for a couple of reasons. The first is my own reaction that morning. On another day, I might have held my breath as well, perceived this man's question as a personal attack and resisted it with apt reasoning on why what I was doing was not the same as his example. Aikido, for instance, is not a religion or belief system. It is a martial art with physical techniques that can be applied in the metaphysical realm. I'm sure I could have made some good points, but in the end I would have lost the participant even if he remained in the class.

Happily, that morning I instinctively blended with his verbal push and aligned with his position. By that I mean that I listened. I also positioned my body so that instead of facing him head-on, I stood at an angle to him. It served the purpose of letting me see the room from his point of view— analogous to what I wanted to accomplish in other ways.

From his perspective, I understood that I was engaging in activity that the culture would not accept from him, and I easily identified with his energy. I might feel the same if I were in his shoes. In that moment, I watched myself make real the aikido metaphor I was teaching. I joined and harnessed his energy. As a result, the encounter had a positive outcome—he stayed and became an active participant. I was grateful for the opportunity to practice what I preach. And, not incidentally, I benefited from a momentary view into a different world.

————·•·————

"Why should I be the first one to yield?"
Sensei Richard Kuboyama's answer ...
"Because you are privileged to have this learning
about flexibility. Others are not so fortunate.
Therefore, it is your responsibility to teach them this
wonderful lesson of nonresistant leading."

– Andy Bryner and Dawna Markova, Ph.D., *An Unused Intelligence*

————·•·————

After the workshop I was moved to think about the deeper implications of this man's question and the resistance that we generally offer to another's strong beliefs about anything. It's true that I was not presenting aikido as dogma, nor did I have expectations that my students would leave professing its values. Consequently, most of the people in the room that day were open to what I had to say.

Still, I had to ask, why do we resist when a fellow worker, friend, or family member speaks to us of God, Jesus, Buddha, Mohammed, or the benefits of living a life based on their teachings? Yes, they are often expressed more vehemently and sometimes with expectations attached. Nevertheless, what could be lost by listening? Why do we defend against the heartfelt beliefs of others, especially in a world that seems to be searching for principles to live by?

Adversarial Listening

There are many reasons of course. Often the energy with which the beliefs are delivered is so strong we feel overwhelmed. Furthermore, if the beliefs are different from our own, we automatically assume we have a conflict. Worried that listening will express tacit agreement, we push back by making counterarguments, changing the subject, or avoiding it altogether.

Adversarial listening takes many forms. While preparing arguments on our own behalf, we tune out the speaker, focusing our mental energy on devising the rebuttal and proving him wrong. If, on the other hand, we decide to avoid the conflict by changing the subject, walking away, or mentally shutting down, we're still making the same arguments to ourselves, just not expressing them. Predictably, the resistance only makes our partner try harder.

When we are listened to, it creates us,
makes us unfold and expand. Ideas actually begin to
grow within us and come to life.

– Brenda Ueland, Author and Journalist

Listening as an Ally

Listening to understand the other's view more clearly is usually not on our list of options. Yet by actively listening to others, we give them and ourselves a great gift. We invite them to let their fountain of energy flow freely. We reinforce their sense of self. We help them find equilibrium and direction. And, surprisingly, it doesn't hurt or compromise us in any way.

Active, connected listening does not mean I will automatically comply with the speaker's request, accept his beliefs, endorse his reasoning, or agree with his viewpoint. It means only that I listen without an agenda and without mentally preparing a rebuttal. This is not an easy task, perhaps in part because I fear learning something that will invite me to change my view. In the most threatening conflicts, my beliefs are challenged and my identity is at risk. If I agree even a little, my sense of being right is threatened. As a result, I don't (*can't*) really listen. This is unfortunate, because when I'm able to listen well, I gain so much.

For example, when I can be wholly present with a speaker, agreement is no longer what's relevant. Instead, I entertain what it would be like to stand in his shoes, see the world from his vantage point, and experience his hopes and fears. Increasingly, I find this a most enjoyable and fascinating endeavor. I gain insight and empathy, increase flexibility and focus, and experience an intimate connection with another person. I hook up with his energy—outrage, joy, excitement, sadness, intense belief—and I identify with his humanness. I realize I've been there, maybe not at this moment, but I've had similar feelings in my life.

You do not need to leave your room.
Remain sitting at your table and listen.
Do not even listen, simply wait.
Do not even wait, be quite still and solitary.
The world will freely offer itself
to you to be unmasked, it has no choice,
it will roll in ecstasy at your feet.

– Franz Kafka

The Art of Listening

You could say that learning to be a good listener is a selfish act. The better listener you are, the more fun you'll have, the more you will find that people want to be around you, and the more you'll learn. It's not always easy, but it is simple: we all benefit from listening more and talking less. The world is growing too complex, too full, and too small not to stop, look, and listen. We can learn a great deal from our "opponents." And when we truly listen as an ally, we discover gifts for ourselves as well.

※

PRACTICE

1. To listen well is an acquired skill. Recall a conversation you had earlier this week in which you wanted to prove your point. How did it go? How might the conversation have gone differently if you had talked less and listened more?

2. Think of a conversation coming up this week where you can explore the art of listening. Practice one or more of the following:

   • Show with body language (head nodding, eye contact) that you are fully present.

   • Quietly vocalize your attention, "uh-huh," "mm-hmm," etc.

   • Summarize the speaker's words occasionally.

   • Guess at the speaker's unstated feelings and hopes. What does he really want?

> • Agree wherever you can. If you have a diverging point
>   of view, wait to bring it up and use it to build on what
>   the speaker offered.
>
> • After you've listened to the other person, summarized
>   his thoughts, and checked to make sure he is finished,
>   you can offer your view of the situation.

MAUREEN'S STORY

*I was at a workshop with Judy on the power of aikido. She talked about
being centered and about embracing instead of resisting. I was quite
impressed to look around the room and hear some very skeptical folks
expressing their intrigue with this "martial art." So practically speaking,
how does one move from a stance of resisting the conflict to a stance of
embracing it? Here is my simple example.*

*A customer of mine comes to inform me of all that is wrong with the
service we have provided. This is a very angry person, nothing has gone
right, and he is expressing a lot of passion about this issue. It has clearly
made a big impact on him, and someone has to fix it.*

*He is positioning for a battle, and I find myself caught without armor.
So I arm myself by listening, really listening. The first thing I find myself
doing is taking it all in and almost pretending it's not about me or us. It's
just a situation that needs to be remedied.*

*Using aikido, I see myself at the side of the "complainer." Whenever I
do this, in every single instance there is something stated that gives me an
opportunity to improve our service. It may be that everything that was
done was appropriate for the situation, but the person beside me had a
different image or expectation of what the service would be. It is amazing
how the picture in front of me changes when I view it as the customer
describes it instead of as I see it.*

Unwanted Guests

This being human is a guest-house
Every morning a new arrival.

– Rumi, Thirteenth-Century Poet and Mystic

I was talking with a friend about feelings. She was saying how unusual and difficult it was for her to express emotions other than happiness. She was brought up to show a joyful demeanor and learned early in life to hide anything else. The world did not need to know when she was upset, anxious, or depressed. Regardless of her actual emotional state, she presented a happy face. Her "front" was perfect.

She became identified with this persona to the extent that she didn't recognize unwanted feelings. She could suppress needs so quickly, she didn't know she had them. It wasn't until a series of unexpected and undesirable events happened in quick succession that she began to lose her ability to achieve this seemingly effortless composure. Because she didn't want to burden others with her problems or appear as anything other than her happy self, she began to stay away from people. Whenever anyone asked how she was, the answer was always "fine."

In time, she found herself in tears at the least provocation. She became more and more depressed and eventually stopped connecting with others altogether. After months of deepening depression, she started to take a look at herself.

She began asking whether it was healthy to quiet all feelings but the "good" ones. She began opening up to close friends and finding other places where she could express herself honestly.

Opening the Floodgates

Does some of this sound familiar? It does to me. I'm not keen on telling others about my problems. I'm supposed to know how to solve them—I teach others how to do it, after all. What might they think if they knew that I, too, get angry, unhappy, or depressed? I'm supposed to be in control all the time, am I not? At emotional times, I imagine myself as a shaky dam barely keeping the river of my feelings from overflowing its banks. Emotions that I consider "too strong" or "unacceptable" press against the restraining barriers of fear and willpower. As time goes on, the pent-up force grows stronger, threatening to burst through and drown everyone within range, including me.

What keeps us from acknowledging our sorrow and our joy, our explosiveness and our sensitivity?

Where's the Gift?

I remember the first time I tried to accept the energy of my anger. Always a challenging emotion, I regarded anger as a threat. It took me away from the nice self I wanted to be and turned me into someone who was pouty, irritable, and impatient. And although I found some short-term pleasure in my crankiness, I knew it was a not-very-useful habit that kept me from communicating in more constructive ways. I decided to try something else. In my angry state, I started running through my usual mental gyrations:

1) I'm angry.

2) I shouldn't be angry, it's not right to be angry.

3) I'm sure they had a good reason for doing what they did.

4) So just let it go.

5) But I can't let it go, I'm still angry!

Round and round I went. I noticed I was arguing with myself. I recognized the *"I shouldn't be angry, it's not right to be angry"* as resistance. I knew from aikido that resistance only causes pushback from whatever it is I'm resisting. The harder I resisted it, the stronger the emotion grew. According to my theory, if I removed the resistance and supported the emotion, it should dissipate.

Invite Them In

To reduce the resistance (to my own emotion) I sat alone and noticed my anger for a while. I observed myself, and I paid attention. The first thing I noticed was how powerful the anger was. It's no wonder I didn't want to feel it. But allowing myself to experience it in this curious, interested way was not overwhelming. Because I wasn't resisting it or hurling it onto anyone, I could feel the power of my emotion in a new (and exciting!) way. As I watched, the intensity diminished.

Gradually I became less driven by the emotion and I became the driver. No longer off balance, I could make better decisions about what to do next. *So this is what it means,* I thought, *to honor my emotions.* Acknowledgment, curiosity, paying attention—I realized that honoring emotions does not mean using them to attack others. It means I become familiar with my emotional energy and use it purposefully.

As I put myself in the driver's seat, I realized I had options. I could have a conversation with the other person without worrying that my emotions would spill over. Or I could wait to see how the emotion played out over the next day or so and what it might teach me. As I began to understand the source of the emotional charge, I was less affected by the problem. I realized that part of the problem was my reaction.

Emotions Happen

When we resist feelings we don't like, they have a way of leaking out and influencing our actions. My friend who identified with her joy and lightness of spirit was afraid to allow conflicting feelings to surface. So they grew in proportion to her resistance, and this emotional imbalance created an internal conflict. As she acknowledged her unexpressed feelings, she regained her balance and more of her self.

Finding ways to manage emotional energy takes awareness, motivation, and practice. It means getting to know our inner voices and feelings, even the ones that are unfamiliar or "unacceptable." And it takes courage. Rather than resisting emotions, get to know them and guide them in useful directions.

PRACTICE

What emotions do you tend to resist? Does the resistance work? How could you put that "resistant" energy to work for you?

Example

- Think of an emotional situation that occurred recently or is about to occur. Listen to your internal dialogue and write it down. Are your thoughts as circular and filled with self-judgment as mine were? Are they critical of the other person? Notice if there's some resistance to owning the emotion.

- Does the resistance show up in physical symptoms, such as a locked jaw, tight stomach, or raised shoulders?

- Separate your position in the conflict from the emotion, and simply acknowledge the power of the emotion. Sit with yourself awhile.

- Can you use your emotional energy in a way that supports your purpose, goals, and vision?

The Guest-House

This being human is a guest-house
Every morning a new arrival.

A joy, a depression, a meanness,
some momentary awareness comes
as an unexpected visitor.

Welcome and entertain them all!
Even if they're a crowd of sorrows,
who violently sweep your house
empty of its furniture.

Still, treat each guest honorably.
He may be clearing you out
for some new delight.

The dark thought, the shame, the malice,
meet them at the door laughing,
and invite them in.

Be grateful for whoever comes,
because each has been sent
as a guide from beyond.

— Rumi, as cited in *Say I Am You: Poetry
Interspersed With Stories of Rumi and Shams,*
translated by John Moyne and Coleman Barks

2

Connection

I connect with the attack.
I accept that a problem exists.
I don't exactly welcome it,
but I am willing to acknowledge
that I have a relationship—
am in relationship—with it.
I realize the connection
was there all along.
I am not separate from the attack
or from the problem.

What separates us
is everything in us
that wants to separate
from each other.
Once you let go
of wanting to separate,
you can begin to see
that we are all one.

— Terry Dobson, *It's A Lot Like Dancing: An Aikido Journey*

Separation is an illusion.
Connectedness is real.

— Thomas Crum, *The Magic of Conflict*

Becoming Each Other

The tree the tempest with a crash of wood
Throws down across our path is not to bar
Our passage to our journey's end for good,
But just to ask us who we think we are ...

– Robert Frost

I love aikido. It's not just something I do, it's a part of me. I
love the energy exchange, the touch, the physical workout,
the perspiring, and the sense of being energized and
exhausted at the same time. I love bowing and saying "thank
you very much," and I love the sense of quiet and peace as
we all sit on the mat waiting for the teacher to begin the
ritual that opens each class. It is a gift in my life. I wake
up mornings thinking how lucky I am to have found it.

One night during a particularly strenuous session, I
suffered a serious soft-tissue injury to my ribs. I stayed off
the mat for about three weeks, hoping to give my body time
to heal, but I didn't wait long enough. Even though I tried
to be careful when I got back on the mat, I could tell I was
straining.

When I sought professional advice, the doctor told me if
I wanted to heal completely, I had to stop practicing aikido
for three months. *Three months!* When you're used to
practicing five days a week, three months seems like a long
time. But I grudgingly folded my practice uniform and sat on
the sidelines, jealously watching my comrades having fun
throwing and being thrown.

Sidelined

I landed on the injured list at a time in my aikido practice that seemed particularly unfair. Having just tested successfully for my black belt, I was in the best physical condition of my life. I was finally feeling my power and using it. It felt great. Then—*boom*—that was it. Sidelined! I was not pleased. But what was I to do? I decided to listen to the doctor and be good. I didn't want to jeopardize my practice, so I took the long view. *Three months isn't forever,* I told myself, *and I will get well and practice again.*

I'm the chief instructor at my school, and although we have other more experienced and gifted teachers, I knew it would not be good for me to be absent for three months. I decided to go to class and observe. So I sat there, quietly missing the energy and the interaction, missing being part of it all. Most of all I missed playing—I missed the sport and fun of practice. I also felt like a wimp. *Others practice with injuries,* I thought. *Why can't I? They'll all think I can't take it—just a girl after all. She hasn't got what it takes.* The internal critic was tough, but I stuck it out.

The View from the Bench

After several nights of sitting on the bench, something changed: I started looking forward to going to class.

At first, the change surprised me. As I watched the students throwing each other, having fun, I noticed myself smiling. Many of the students were new to aikido, and they all seemed to love it. The longer I watched, the more joy I derived from the experience. I would see little things—a kind gesture extended by one partner to another, a smile, a laugh at a technique gone awry; a senior student gently using the movement of his body to show a new person how the technique might be done more smoothly; a young boy doing one forward roll after another to figure out why he crunches his shoulder on one side but not the other, another senior student trying to help him figure it out.

The more classes I watched, the more I began to see things I never would have seen while practicing or teaching. I began to see the exchange of energy that I missed so much—alive and in the flesh. Putting power into a partner who is capable of receiving it is an awesome feeling. Receiving another's energy is equally incredible. *Here is power, here is some of me, take it,* offers one partner. *Give me your power, give me all you've got—I can take it,* says the other. They were not using words but physical actions. I watched this exchange happen over and over again, a hundred times in an hour's practice. And it seemed to go beyond even the physical. As they extended their energy, they extended themselves—their essences—nothing less. What are we but energy? You take a little bit of me, and I receive something of you.

———

**Work in the invisible world
at least as hard
as you do in the visible.**

– Rumi

———

Energy Exchange

As new students step onto the mat and join this community of energy, they enter with their own attitudes and beliefs, their physical and non-physical power. Attitudes of fear or cockiness gradually join in, blend, and are transformed by the exchange of energy that takes place every time we touch one another. Newcomers become more like us, and we like them. We blend and unite. As I watched this giving and receiving of power, the thought that came to mind was, *we are becoming each other.*

Is it so different off the mat? In life, when we shake hands, embrace, speak to one another, touch our partners with our bodies or our words, are we not in some invisible way exchanging a piece of our selves? Knowing this, will I make different choices?

I would not have chosen to be sidelined for such a long time and indeed often railed against it. But I also see that I was permitted a new level of practice. Life threw me into a fall for which I was not prepared, but I gradually found my center and rolled out of it.

The view from the bench was unexpected and fascinating. I may sit there again *just because.* As I silently witnessed the gentle, kind, playful, and powerful souls in front of me, I experienced hope. It isn't hard to imagine that soon we will all come to understand we are not separate. We are connected by invisible strands of energy, and we are becoming more aware of that connection daily. The bench offered a beautiful view and a gift that surprised and changed me. Thank you very much.

Life throws things at us that we cannot predict and cannot control.
What we can control is who we are along the way.

– Philip Simmons, *Learning to Fall*

PRACTICE

1. Think of a problem or situation that occurred in your past, one that at the time seemed insurmountable or created a huge barrier to what you were going for.

   - How did you find your way out of the situation?

   - Did it permit you a different level of "practice" in your life? A different view?

   - In retrospect, how do you experience what came about because of the obstacle?

2. What is your current obstacle? Is there a purpose behind this situation that your resistance is preventing you from seeing?

CHRISTINE'S STORY

I was watching television late one night when I heard a car horn honking over and over again outside my apartment window. My anger flared immediately. I got up, ran to the door, and began to shout at the woman in the car to stop. The honking continued. Normally, I would have run out in my bathrobe and started to bang on the car window—or worse. I've got a well-earned reputation for having a hot temper and "an attitude"! I would have told the woman off in no uncertain terms and perhaps done more than that. But I'd learned about centering earlier that day and thought I'd try it out, just to see.

As I centered myself, I began to wonder why the woman continued to honk the horn with such a regular rhythm and considered for the first time that something might be wrong. I went out to the car and tapped lightly on the window, which the woman rolled down. She didn't look well. I asked if she was okay, and she said no, she thought her pulse was fast. She went on to say she didn't know where she was and asked if someone could get help, which I promptly did. With the woman safely in the proper care, I felt good that I'd taken a moment to connect with myself and change my perspective.

Relax!

The environment is invented by our presence in it.

– Margaret J. Wheatley and Myron Kellner-Rogers, *A Simpler Way*

Relax—a word often heard during aikido practice.

"Relax!" says the teacher. "Relax!" I say to my partner. "Relax. Don't be so stiff. You're working too hard. It's much easier than that." It's all true. And if only I could take my own advice.

The parallels between my aikido practice and daily life appear to be limitless. One that shows up everywhere relates to relaxation. I tend to give a lot of advice on the mat. I'm often the teacher and I'm supposed to advise, but I also do it when I'm practicing—when I'm just somebody's partner. For example, I might suggest that my partners relax if I sense that they are stiff, resistant, or generally making the technique more difficult than it needs to be. I try to demonstrate where they are tense or struggling. My intention is to support, but maybe there's a better way.

There is no question aikido is a martial art that takes a lifetime to master. A typical reaction in the face of attack is to tighten up against the oncoming assault. One of the most important reasons for practicing aikido is to learn a different way. If students can "relax" and not stiffen or freeze, they can move out of the way of an attack and be in a better position to connect with the attacker's energy. This relaxed, energized blending is the essence of power. It is why we practice aikido, but it is also one of the most difficult tasks to master—on the mat or off.

So here I am telling my "stiff" partner to relax and take it easy, but what about me? My arms are more relaxed than his perhaps, but I can still feel strain. I'm holding my breath, and my center has moved up into my shoulders. I seem to have "caught" some tension from my partner. The more he stiffens, the tighter I become, especially as I attempt to "correct" him. *He's not falling right! If he'd only loosen up a little, he could feel what I want him to do! Oh, he'll never get it. He's just too tight.*

A Change of Focus

Out of curiosity, I move my focus to my own body instead of my partner's, wondering if this "contagiousness" might work in reverse. Because I become tense in response to my partner's stiffness, maybe if I relax, he will, too. I try, and it works. As I become more relaxed, so does my partner.

I begin to ask myself which one of us needed the admonition to relax. At the same time, I comprehend the depth of the connection between us. I see that it only takes one of us to make a change that both of us experience. I reflect on whether our newfound relaxation might radiate beyond our small sphere and have an effect on the other students. It's possible.

—·—

***We and our environments become one system, each influencing the
other, each co-determining the other.***

– Margaret J. Wheatley and Myron Kellner-Rogers, *A Simpler Way*

—·—

Off the Mat

If this "relaxation contagion" works on the mat, maybe it
works off the mat, too. One of my students told me she uses
it in the dentist's chair. "Tensing all my muscles makes the
experience so much worse, and learning to relax really is
helpful. When I breathe and exhale, I think the dentist
relaxes a little, too," she said.

We mirror the physical tension we see in others. If you
doubt this, the next time you feel tense, notice if there is
someone nearby who is tense. As you relax, watch to see if
that person also relaxes. The applications of this model are
limited only by your imagination. When your life-partner
starts shouting at you or the kids, instead of shouting back,
relax and regain control of yourself and the situation. When
you notice that your boss is tense (again!), instead of bracing
yourself against the coming onslaught, relax and see how the
change is reflected in the environment. When you ask your
15-year-old to clean that room now (!) and see her stiffen,
relax and invite her to help you figure out what you can
both do to resolve the ongoing struggle.

We often hear it said that we cannot control others, and
for the most part, that is true. We cannot force others to be

the way we want them to be. But because we are in relationship with them, because we're connected, they will be affected by our choice to breathe and become more centered.

A Different Kind of Control

We are used to controlling others with force. If I am bigger and stronger, I can control you. If I'm a parent or a boss, I can tell you what to do, and you have to obey (for a while anyway). We use power to control.

In aikido practice, I gain a different kind of control by practicing a relaxed, energized countenance in the face of attack. I relax, move, and engage the energy coming toward me. I control myself so that I can guide the attacker. By moving in harmony with my partner's movements, I feel where his energy is going, which affects what I do next. Depending on how he moves, I adjust. I find power through flexibility, which begins with physical relaxation. I blend, connect, and redirect.

In non-physical aikido, you do the same thing: relax, blend, connect, and redirect from moment to moment, making choices that return you to your vision of who you are and where you are going.

It's not easy—or rather it takes practice. But, just like aikido on the mat, off-the-mat aikido is powerful and fun once you learn the techniques.

PRACTICE

1. Think of a person at work who needs to relax.

   • The next time this person is near you, notice if you become tense. What specific areas of your body are tight? How is your breathing?

   • Next, begin to relax, center, and breathe. Gradually feel your shoulders lower, your jaw unlock, and your knees relax. How does your relaxation affect you, your co-worker, and your relationship?

2. Be attentive to your body today. Notice when you hold your breath or tighten your muscles. How are you right now? Is there tension anywhere in your body? If so, focus on that spot. Breathe into it, and as you exhale, release the tension. As the day unfolds, be aware of physical tension creeping in, focus on it, and let it go. If there are others with you, notice if they relax, too. As you learn to let go of physical tension, you'll find your mind and spirit will also free up.

JACK'S STORY

An issue that keeps coming up for me is how I resist certain behaviors in other people, only to find out—somewhere down the road—that I'm doing the very same thing. I realize how much time and energy I'm wasting wishing "they" would change.

Turn Signals and Enlightenment

i am through you so i

– e. e. cummings

"We are all one" is a familiar and wise saying that I happen to believe is true, and lately I've been experiencing it firsthand.

For example, on a recent drive down a central thoroughfare in my home city of Portsmouth, New Hampshire, I was getting ready to make a right turn onto a side street, and I forgot to activate my turn signal. Another car was waiting at the stop sign on that side street—the one I was turning onto—getting ready to enter my street. The driver waited for me to pass by, not knowing I intended to turn since I gave him no indication. Of course, I realized afterward that the driver could have entered my street earlier had I signaled. I remembered the times I'd been in that driver's place and silently cursed an oncoming car for not signaling. In my mind's eye, I experienced myself cursing myself—a peculiar moment.

The following week, I was driving on a main artery in a nearby town, gazing out my car window at the lovely sky as traffic crept along at a snail's pace. I suddenly became aware of someone wanting to pull in front of me from the lane on my left. The driver was in the left-turn-only lane but didn't want to turn left. Realizing his error, he quickly tried to merge so he could continue straight through the light ahead. He was upset because I didn't immediately notice and make room, and the look he gave me—well, let's say it was daggers. I became upset, too. After all, I simply didn't see him. Then I remembered my own teaching, took a deep breath, centered myself, and let him in.

---

*Each time we get back in touch with ourselves,
conditions become favorable for us
to encounter life in the present moment.*

– Thich Nhat Hanh, Vietnamese Poet and Monk

Maybe he saw my smile, I don't know, but he seemed to calm down. And then I realized, *Wait a minute! That could have been me in that car.* I've been there, had those feelings: *Wrong lane, oops! I gotta get over, but she won't brake for me. Hmmmph!* I saw myself in the mirror again.

Reflections

I've had many mini-awakenings like this. I keep seeing myself in other people—other angry people, frustrated people, silly, judgmental, frightened, and, thankfully, happy people. No sooner do I start to criticize my neighbor for some act of stupidity than I remember, *I've done that.* And I see my own reflection. I appreciate the feelings the other person is experiencing as I remember my own. In a very real sense I *am* that person.

Watching people ahead of me in a long line at the Store24 near my home, I see impatience, frustration, boredom, and amusement as I look from face to face. But instead of looking from the outside in judgment, I'm feeling from the inside with compassion for our common condition—the human condition. The result is that I'm becoming less critical of others and of myself. This new awareness grows and intensifies like a reinforcing loop: the less I am critical of others, the less I critique myself, and the less I critique myself, the less I am critical of others.

Choose Wisely

But there's more. As I identify with the actions of others, I also identify with their attitude toward me. In this reflexive view of relationship, what I say or do to another I am quite literally saying or doing to myself. I notice the angry thought toward the driver who forgets to signal her turn, and it's like I'm sending it to myself. Do I want to do that? As I tune into the Universal Wisdom Channel, the reality of the mantra that "we are all one" really hits home.

In many of his residential programs, author and teacher Thomas Crum guides participants in a *tai chi* movement called *Embrace Tiger, Return to Mountain*. In its slow and lovely dancelike motions, it suggests we embrace all of life as a gift. One gesture represents how our actions and thoughts create our world and that what we offer out to the universe will indeed come back to visit us. We choose and we extend—our energy, our being—with every breath. And as I have discovered in the conflict laboratory of my car, it's important to choose wisely.

PRACTICE

Remember a time recently when you had an angry moment
and said or did something you wish you hadn't.

Close your eyes and go back to that moment.
Replay the scene—this time breathing, relaxed, centered,
and calm. As you envision the incident, what would you do
differently? How does the scene play out this time?

Visualizing and replaying scenes in this way will help you
practice and reinforce the centered state.

JERI'S STORY

*During my morning commute into Boston, I was stuck in traffic. I was not
particularly upset about the traffic because I expected it. I was at a red light
and wanted to merge into the right lane. Hoping that someone would let
me in, I started to inch over. A guy in a pickup passed me, not letting me
into the lane. As he passed, he waved his arms at me, probably swearing
angrily that I had the nerve to merge in front of him. I merged into the lane
directly behind him.*

*I began to react to his reaction and was angry with him for being angry
with me. I almost yelled back. But then I thought, "It's a beautiful summer
day. I'm not in a rush, and why should he ruin my morning?" So instead, I
looked at him in his rear-view mirror. I smiled peacefully and thought things
like, "Good morning. I hope you have a great day, because it is too beautiful
to have a bad day."*

*I think he got a little uncomfortable. He was not expecting pleasantness
after his outburst. I felt a little strange continuing to smile, but by the time the
light turned green, he was waving at me as if to say, "Bye, have a nice day."
Or maybe it was his way of apologizing! I thought to myself, "That was fun!"*

3

Practice

As I acknowledge
my connection to the problem,
I begin to engage and understand it.
I take action and
learn from the outcome.
As with a new musical instrument,
I perfect and polish my technique
until there is no technique.
I am the instrument.
I practice, and I improve.

Work. Keep digging your well.
Don't think about getting off from work.
Water is there somewhere.

Submit to a daily practice.
Your loyalty to that
is a ring on the door.

Keep knocking, and the joy inside
will eventually open a window
and look out to see who's there.

— Rumi, as cited in *One-Handed Basket Weaving: Rumi Poems*
on the Theme of Work, versions by Coleman Barks

Getting on the Mat

Practice makes perfect.

– Proverb

A tourist stops a New Yorker on the street and asks, "How do you get to Carnegie Hall?" The New Yorker replies: "Practice!" An old joke, but a good one.

Students of aikido often part saying, "See you on the mat!" Essentially this implies, "I'll see you at practice," but it holds a wealth of meaning for the practitioner that might not be readily apparent to others. It means: we know we're in this for the long run, we'll never be masters, we'll be practicing all our lives, and we know how grueling and fun and hard and endless and enduring and energizing it is.

"See you on the mat" means: see you at the place where we all learn and develop together; where learning never stops; where we learn by falling down and getting up again a hundred times a night; where we run into our own egos, deficiencies, physical limitations, and better selves; and where we also find miraculous moments of power, clarity, and connection. It's all there on the mat.

"Getting on the mat" means I'm willing to practice and take on all that goes with it. I'm willing to try, fail, try again, fail again, and eventually reach a new level of skill, where I'll remain awhile until, by continually getting on the mat, practicing, trying, failing, and learning, I reach another level and yet another. There is no end. The black belt means I'm

starting a new phase of my development and I'm ready to be
a beginner again.

Practice Makes Perfect

"Getting on the mat" is relevant to numberless "off the mat"
experiences in our day-to-day lives. We figuratively get on
the mat when we engage in a difficult conversation, attempt
to resolve a conflict, try out a new tact with a disrespectful
employee, or go another round with a teenage son or
daughter.

On the aikido mat, I know that if I want to get better at
something, I have to practice. It's the same with our daily
disputes, small and large. The advantage of learning a martial
art is that I have a place I can go that is designed specifically
for practice. Four to five days a week, I literally *get on the mat*
with other like-minded students and practice throwing,
pinning, and falling, again and again. I learn how to protect
myself and be resilient, adaptable, and calm under pressure.
Over time, the constant repetition of mental and physical
techniques begins to take hold. I improve.

Whatever you would make habitual, practice it;
and if you would not make a thing habitual, do not practice it,
but accustom yourself to something else.

– Epictetus, First-Century Greek Philosopher

By practicing skills for handling our skirmishes at home and
at work, we can improve in similar ways. In place of rigid
attitudes, we can practice flexibility and centered presence.
Instead of being thrown by conflict, we can expand our

capacity to move, adapt, and change, instantaneously responding to the needs of the moment. And instead of being stuck in fear, we can learn to cultivate awareness, and trust that our intuition and vision will support us.

But the reality is that the only time we practice coping with conflict is when we're actually in one. Staying with the aikido metaphor for a moment, this strikes me as inadequate preparation, similar to observing a few aikido techniques and then being thrust onto the mat with four experienced attackers.

Not the best method for learning.

Yet this is exactly how we confront conflict most of the time—unprepared and suddenly in performance mode. *How did this happen? How did I get here?* It's not surprising we tend to avoid conflict. Nor is it surprising that we rarely see conflict handled well. Yet when it is, like the beautiful, dancing movements of aikido, conflict transformation can be breathtaking.

Conflict Habits

Because we lack preparation, we often apply the wrong techniques when we are thrust onto the metaphorical mat. Conflict arises, and we do *something*. Unfortunately, if we are unskilled, we end up reinforcing our personal conflict "habits"—unconscious and reactive behavior patterns—that are often ineffective, inappropriate, or harmful. The problem is that we're not practiced at anything else, so we continue to fall back on these habitual reactions, even if they don't produce the desired result.

Many of us try to change these patterns. We do our best to learn new responses. We may even take courses and acquire specific new skills. But after the course is over, when we're back at home, in the office, or at the bargaining table and things get hot, we tend to do what we've always done.

How use doth breed a habit...

– William Shakespeare

Going to the Dojo

To develop new skills and use them consistently, we have to "get on the mat." We have to practice. Good courses, books, and coaches offer a place to start. Then it's up to us, which means commitment to a new vision, disciplined pursuit of the goal, and the courage to try out our new techniques. It also helps to find places where we can practice safely.

The Japanese word *dojo* means "place of practice," and it is in the dojo, on the mat, where we learn aikido and where we can make the mistakes essential to learning. Where do you practice? Do you have a "mat" where you can try out new skills, make mistakes, and practice improving your technique?

My "mat" is a group of friends. We've agreed to partner with each other when we need to practice. We role-play and offer feedback on current conflicts or on ones we've experienced and wish we'd handled differently. We help each other gain insight and competence.

You can also practice in actual conflict situations with minimal risk, such as the petty annoyances that occur throughout the day. You're in a hurry, and you can't find your briefcase. Stop. Take a deep breath, and exhale slowly. Center yourself. You'll find your briefcase faster, and you have just begun to establish a useful new habit.

Another way to practice new behavior is to look for skillful role models—people you admire because of the way they handle adversity. Watch them, emulate their actions, and adopt their attitude toward life.

Practice Under Pressure

The more often you practice, the more prepared you'll feel when something more challenging comes along. Whatever the outcome of the conflict, one of the best methods for continued improvement is to reflect on your actions after the conflict is over. Ask two questions:

• What did I do well?

• What would I do differently next time?

Make it a point to find at least one thing you did well. Then mentally replay the scene the way you would like to do it next time.

Invisible Habits

A teacher once told me that you know you've acquired a new habit when it becomes as invisible as the old one. If you're asking how long this process will take, ask yourself how long it took to become skilled at the last new hobby you took up. How long did it take to be trained in your job? If you're conscientious and committed, you may see change in a very short time. But the learning never really ends.

Life contains conflict, and learning to handle it gracefully is a lifetime pursuit, so be easy with yourself and find ways to enjoy your practice. You don't become a black belt in a day, nor do you change your conflict habits easily or quickly. If you want to replace old habits with new ones, get on the mat and start practicing. Carnegie Hall is just down the street.

*To truly recognize and understand the way of aikido may require
spending an entire lifetime and an enormous amount of energy.*

— Mitsunari Kanai, *Technical Aikido*

PRACTICE

How will you practice? It's best to start with the basics,
like centering. The advantage to starting with a centering
practice is that you can do it anywhere, anytime.
When you're in the centered state, you are calm,
in control of yourself, and able to choose from
many useful options.

1. **Ways to begin a centering practice.**

   • **Center now.** You can train yourself to center by
   standing in a relaxed posture and directing the weight
   of your body toward your physical center—an internal
   point about an inch and a half below your navel.
   Breathe into this center point of your body. Breathe
   out from this same point. You will begin to feel more
   composed, confident, and in charge of yourself, both
   physically and emotionally.

   Breathe consciously, and feel the air flow easily
   through your nose, head, throat, lungs, and deep into
   your abdomen. Hear the sound the breath makes,
   and feel it as it flows in and out. Sit quietly for a few
   minutes and relax your mind. You can do this

anytime. Athletes recognize the centered state as "the zone." Some say it is an attitude toward life, an ability to handle whatever may come.

- **Start your day centered.** Physical exercise, deep breathing, meditation, prayer, and quiet reflection are tried and true centering practices. You may have your own. By starting your day with a centering activity, you will return to the centered state more easily as the day's events unfold.

- **Create centering triggers.** Triggers are objects, behaviors, people, or events that remind you to re-center periodically. Place posters or quotations on the wall that reinforce your vision. Keep a book of affirmations close at hand or a picture of a loved one to help you remember what is really important. Listen to one of your favorite centering tapes as you drive to and from work. When you push open the door to your office, let it be a trigger to center yourself.

- **Practice on little things.** Find something in your normal routine and make it a centering practice. Do it for thirty days, keep track, and be specific. For example: each time the phone rings, I will take a breath and exhale before I answer it.

  My thirty-day practice:

  _____

  _____

  _____

  _____

  _____

2. **Ways to continue your practice.**

- **Use conflict as an opportunity to practice.** When everything seems to be falling apart, breathe into your center point. Regain balance and perspective.

- **Create a list of possible support people.** These are the people with whom you can practice conflict scenarios when the need arises. Call someone and practice.

  Support people:

  _____

  _____

  _____

  _____

- **Find a role model.** Think of one or two people you admire for the way they handle conflict, adversity, or difficult conversations. Watch them, and consider scheduling a time to talk with them.

  People I admire:

  _____

  _____

  _____

  _____

BOB'S STORY

The power of centering is, indeed, a real thing and manifests itself in tangible ways. The first time I met with Judy, she gave me a few simple exercises to show me what centering felt like. Shortly afterward I went to the bank and then to a store. I took the opportunity to practice centering just before opening each door, and I was pleasantly surprised at the reactions I received from strangers. Normally I pay little attention to the people I interact with or share space with in stores. On this occasion, I felt centered, and total strangers smiled and said hi to me. My banking and shopping experiences were definitely enhanced that day. After that experience, I decided to consciously test to see if centering would elicit warm responses in other situations.

I frequently attend meetings where I am just one face in a sea of faces, all watching a few speakers at the podium. I practiced centering while listening to the speakers and noticed something remarkable. Ordinarily I would watch the speaker's eyes cast about the hall and almost never land on me. But when I centered, I discovered that the speakers began making and holding eye contact with me. I had changed nothing else—not the location of my seat, my facial expression, or anything except the feeling of being centered. When I became consciously aware of this contact, I would become distracted by the success of my test and lose the speaker's attention. Then I would re-center and regain the speaker's attention. This has happened so repeatedly that I am now convinced that whatever it is centering does for me, it is also apparent to other people in my sphere.

There are many exercises I can perform during my workday that alert me to find my center. For example, I used to have a very negative reaction to the telephone, since it is always an interruption and often an unpleasant one. Now I use the first ring of the phone to signal me to take a breath and go to my center. Then I answer after the second ring—and I have even had people comment on how calm I seem to be when answering the phone.

Keeping Conflict in Perspective

I'm sorry to say so
but, sadly, it's true
that Bang-ups
and Hang-ups
can happen to you.

– Dr. Seuss, *Oh, the Places You'll Go!*

A friend told me about a conflict she was having with her next door neighbor. Because of a misunderstanding, the neighbor was pretty upset, so much so that when they passed on the street and my friend said hello and reached out to shake hands, he withdrew his. He avoided eye contact, muttered a monotone "hi," and quickly walked past her.

She felt as if she'd been punched in the stomach. Stunned, she walked back to her house wondering what had just happened. It was even more upsetting because she had communicated with this man about the confusion that had initially caused the conflict, and she thought he understood her point of view. She wanted to find out what went wrong, but he clearly didn't want to discuss it. We talked about the incident for a while, brainstorming strategies that would help her deal with this unexpected blow, but eventually I left her to think it over on her own.

———•————

You'll get mixed up, of course,
as you already know.
You'll get mixed up
with many strange birds as you go.

– Dr. Seuss, *Oh, the Places You'll Go!*

———•————

Surprise Attack

A surprise attack is one of the hardest conflicts to handle. It's a shock to the system. Often the first reaction (after your heartbeat returns to normal) is to blame the other person or yourself and to get caught in endless internal dialogue about who's at fault and what to do next.

Regardless of the cause, a troubling conflict may take time to resolve and can disrupt life while it's going on. In the confusion, we lose our center and often operate on half-power, the other half working non-stop to figure out where to assign blame and (as much as possible) to justify our actions. It can be so disturbing that we lose focus, have difficulty making even routine decisions, and spend wakeful nights deliberating over the best way to solve the problem. It's hard to do anything wholeheartedly until the conflict is resolved.

I felt a lot of empathy for my friend with the disgruntled neighbor. I've been there, and it's no fun. One of the ways I tried to help was to listen when she needed to talk. I also suggested she take care of herself while trying to untangle this knotty situation. Conflict is hard on the body, on the mind, and on the spirit, especially when it catches you by surprise. In his book, *Why Zebras Don't Get Ulcers,* Robert Sapolsky gives clear evidence and many examples of the effects of stress on the cardiovascular, digestive, and immune systems, as well as its connection with depression, personality, and temperament. Activation of the stress response releases numerous hormones that affect our ability to eat, sleep, think, speak, work, rest, and suppress disease.

How can you prepare when you don't know the conflict is coming? And how can you regain your inner and outer balance?

———•———

So be sure when you step.
Step with care and great tact
and remember that Life's
a Great Balancing Act.

– Dr. Seuss, *Oh, the Places You'll Go!*

———•———

You're on the Mat, Now What?

As you go through your daily activities, employ these mental and physical strategies to help restore perspective, reduce your body's stress response, and move the conflict toward a positive resolution.

• **Breathe and center.** Often. A conflict can unbalance us with strong emotions and feelings of unworthiness, anger, sadness, and frustration. Don't avoid your emotions, but treat them as guides. Appreciate and observe them as you might observe a play. There is a lot of power in this emotional energy, and as you breathe, center, and watch, you'll discover how to use your emotions in a way that is in line with your best purpose.

- **Take the long view.** It's so easy to get caught in the turmoil of the conflict that we forget there will be a tomorrow. Take some quiet moments to close your eyes and see yourself in the future with the conflict resolved. Imagine how you'll feel with the problem behind you. What would you like the relationship to look like a month from now? A year from now? Meanwhile, eat well, go to bed at regular hours, laugh, and allow yourself to forget the problem occasionally. This may not be easy, but it's effective. Allow your inner wisdom to work silently while you continue to engage in life.

- **Reframe.** Step outside the conflict momentarily and look at it through a more objective lens. Instead of resisting, ask yourself if there is a gift here—an invitation to look at things differently or to try a new behavior. Acknowledge the other person by standing in his shoes. Why is he behaving this way? What does he want? How would you feel in his position?

- **Experiment.** Brainstorm all possible responses to this situation and try them on for size. Ask a friend to role-play alternatives you think you'd never choose because they're so unlike your usual persona. Have fun exercising unexplored selves.

- **Practice.** Choose one new behavior that will make a positive difference in your attitude toward life and make a commitment to practice that behavior everyday.

- **Count your blessings.** Notice the good things in your life. Cultivate gratitude and wonder.

Conflict can cause us to lose sight of the big picture—of what we truly want in life, why we're here, and what is important in a particular relationship—or to see it more clearly. Get on the mat and engage the conflict energy. Work with it and move it in a positive, useful direction. Meeting life in this way is the key to finding your true power.

————

And will you succeed?
Yes! You will, indeed!
(98 and ¾ percent guaranteed.)

– Dr. Seuss, *Oh, the Places You'll Go!*

————

After brainstorming many options, my friend decided to write a letter to her neighbor. She refrained from justifying her own actions. Instead, she acknowledged his feelings and offered to talk with him about the situation. Her letter opened up a renewed conversation and, over time, they came to be good neighbors again.

PRACTICE

What happens to you physically and emotionally
when you're surprised by conflict?

How do you usually behave, and how is it different
from what you would like to do?

Recall the last time you experienced
this kind of "surprise attack."

How did you handle it?

What did you do well?

What might you have done differently?

What next steps will you take?

SCOTT'S STORY

Last summer, my father and I had a big fight. I had just finished spending a weeklong vacation with friends at our summer cottage. At the end of the week, we were cleaning the cottage when Dad showed up. He was very angry and accused my friends and me of dumping garbage up the road instead of taking it with us. I tried to explain that it wasn't our garbage, but Dad wouldn't listen and screamed at me in front of my friends.

It's amazing how quickly a middle-aged man turns into an angry teenager when old wounds are reopened.

I barely spoke to my father for several months. When he did call, I was terse and ended our conversations as quickly as possible. I could not let go of my anger and embarrassment. I felt that if I gave in, I would be justifying my father's actions.

Then I remembered your advice about getting close to the conflict. The next time my father called, I told him why I had been short with him the past few months. I explained why I was upset: his refusal to believe the truth, his decision to embarrass me in front of my friends, and his refusal to listen to me at all.

My father listened and apologized. I'm not going to say that this was the first time he ever said he was sorry, but it was close. Our relationship has continued to improve since then.

Ah, Yes ... Another Sporting Event

From discord, find harmony.
In the middle of difficulty, lies opportunity.

– Albert Einstein

On a beautiful Saturday morning, I found myself upset with my husband. Jim was reading the sports page and remarking on the abundance of quality televised events. He said jokingly, "You don't have somewhere to go today, do you?" In case you're not married to a sports fan, let me make the implication perfectly clear. He was humorously referring to the fact that he hoped to watch TV sports all day, guilt-free.

I knew exactly what he meant, and doubtless, another time I might have heard the joke and laughed at it. But not that day. Receiving the comment as a reflection on how good a wife and companion I was, I became angry and hurt. What I felt in the moment was: *How dare you say that! I never complain when you watch sports on television. I'm the best wife in the world about that stuff, and you know it!*

In an earlier life, I would have gone off in a huff, righteously enjoying my rightness. Instead I took a breath and centered myself. I didn't want to fight about this. But I did want to communicate and express my view that the joke was not in line with reality—mine at least. I said, "That's not very nice." He explained he was only joking and that he doesn't even watch sports that much. I knew by the sound of his voice that now he was upset, too. We were on the cusp of an attitude war: Jim needing to prove he was a good husband, and I needing to prove I was a good wife. It was my move. I centered again.

It's amazing how much power there is in a moment like this. It was a non-event, really, yet one that could go either way. He was right. He doesn't actually watch sports that much, and it's one of the ways he relaxes after a long workweek. And I was right. I hardly ever complain about television.

I took a breath, centered myself, and said, "I know you're only joking, and I know you know I don't mind your watching sports." It wasn't what I said as much as the attitude shift I made. Instead of blaming, I acknowledged his side and mine. He said, "I know you don't mind, and I really appreciate it." I said I knew this, too. As we acknowledged the truth in each other's statements, we also found our positive intentions and were back on track for a good Saturday that would have some time for TV, sports, and relationship.

———•—•———

***Just as fast as a fish can move in water,
you can instantly move to a happy, balanced attitude.***

– Tarthang Tulku Rinpoche

———•—•———

Why Should I Change?

This attitude shift, when it happens, answers the important question, "Why should *I* be the one to change?" In this case, I did it for myself. In seconds, I realized I didn't want to spend the day, or even an hour, grumpy and mad. So I made a choice that helped move the budding conflict in a more positive direction. As a participant in one of my workshops put it, to be willing to change can be an act of self-love.

Perhaps the willingness to entertain change is change. I altered my view of the conflict and gained a new perspective. I did not engage that part of me that wanted to fight, to prove I was right, or to win, because it was not useful then. It did not serve my purpose of reestablishing connection. As I made the shift, I engaged the self that values the relationship over the contest, the me that is wise. I established a new relationship to the conflict and was able to guide it in a more purposeful direction.

Attitude Adjustment

As I see it, all conflict comes down to whether I'm willing to make this internal shift and revolves around the question: am I willing to change? In this question lies the magic and power of human will and consciousness.

———

Consciousness is the most stubborn substance in the cosmos, and the most fluid. It can be rigid as concrete, and it can change in an instant.

– Starhawk, *The Fifth Sacred Thing*

———

71

In the spirit of experimentation and practice, I've been testing my ability to shift my attitude. For example, I might try a new attitude on for size because the current one isn't useful. I'm at a party and find myself judging all the partygoers. As I shift to curiosity, the party becomes more interesting.

At times I pretend what it would be like to have a different attitude, even if I can't exactly go there in the moment. If I'm nervous about a client meeting, for example, I take a moment to imagine a person who is not nervous but confident and skilled at establishing rapport. I'm fascinated to find that person alive and well in me, and she enables me to be present during the ensuing conversation.

These "invisible" moments, when approached with consciousness, have the power to turn a situation around and help me go forward with purpose. As I practice self-awareness, I increase my comfort level with conflict and my ease in leading it to a beneficial outcome.

There is a basket of fresh bread on your head,
and yet you go door to door asking for crusts.
Knock on your inner door.

– Rumi

Does This Count?

Sometimes Jim kids me about whether the time we spend together counts as "relationship time." For instance, does watching television together count? Or is it only when we're engaged in deep conversation? In the context of the awareness and courage it takes to manage these conscious shifts in attitude, it's all about relationship, and it all counts.

✳

PRACTICE

Looking back on the week, recall any moments in which you made a conscious choice to shift to a more useful perspective or attitude.

Now bring to mind a moment where this kind of internal shift might have been a good idea, but you couldn't or wouldn't make it. How would you describe your self in that instance? In retrospect, why did you not make the shift, and what did you learn?

JAN'S STORY

I have a new, very bright employee whom I've been gradually trying to bring up to speed on business practices, so as not to overwhelm her. She came up with her own business plan, which took me completely by surprise. In fact, when I opened the email with her suggestions, I felt as if I had been kicked in the stomach. I read her note as an indictment of our business style and felt pretty angry about it. My first response was to sit down and talk to her about what I perceived as the inappropriateness of her actions, and I got in the car and headed toward our office to have the conversation.

On the hourlong drive, I had time to think, and before long the aikido approach to conflict came into my mind. Sure enough, I began to understand that this woman was probably trying to help and better the situation for the company. I still didn't like her telling me what to do, but I appreciated where her efforts came from—even if it still sounded like criticism. Ultimately, I stepped back from my first response to confront her (and tell her to back off) and decided to back off myself. I took the rest of the day off and gave myself a break from the whole issue.

4

Discovery

The attack is reconfigured as
I change my attitude toward it.
I engage resources I didn't know I had.
Where I was resistant, now I'm interested.
Instead of being judgmental, I am curious.
What does life look like to others?
How does the world, in all its wonder,
cross the threshold of another's experience?

*The universe is
asking me to open to
new perspectives
that are limited only
by my willingness
to engage my
imagination.*

– Author

Life Is What You Make It

"Hope" is the thing with feathers –
That perches in the soul –
And sings the tune without the words –
And never stops – at all –

– Emily Dickinson

My Aunt Mimi was a teacher, mentor, second mother, and bright spirit in my life. By her side I learned knitting, sewing, the social graces, and much more: I learned how to flow with what life offers.

Looking back, I see my 12-year-old self working the pedal of Mimi's old, black Singer sewing machine. She's beside me, watching approvingly and giving gentle hints. In another scene, I'm having a manicure. Mimi is delicately filing each of my fingernails.

Then it's Christmas Eve at my grandparents' house—Mimi lived with them—and I'm opening a present from her. It's a "Handmade by Mimi" poodle skirt with a beautiful felt cutout design. All the girl cousins receive one, and we immediately put them on and start twirling. Another Christmas, Mimi's gifts to us are full-length red flannel nightgowns with white lace at the collar and white buttons down the front. They will keep us warm until we outgrow them. One year she sews tiny, perfect red-checked dresses and white crinoline pinafores for our eight-inch Madame Alexander dolls.

Life Lessons

Mimi took us to the movies, on walks around the neighborhood, and shopping downtown. A bunch of cousins would pile into her car and she'd drive us to Play Land—an amusement park where we would ride the Ferris wheel and eat cotton candy while she looked on.

Mimi helped me pick out my first mini-skirt and then stood by when my father saw it and hit the roof. It was the first time in my life that I was able to express what I was feeling to my dad, because Mimi said, "Go ahead, Judy, talk to your father. What do you want to say?"

————•——

Angels appreciate things about you that you thought no one else ever noticed.

– Anonymous

————•——

What I haven't told you is that Mimi lived most of her life in a wheelchair. At 13, she was a normal teenager who played the piano, sang, took ballet class, and was active in school plays. The third of five children of Greek immigrant parents, she got top grades, had lots of friends, and enjoyed good health and high spirits.

When she began to experience pain in her back in 1934, physicians couldn't find the cause. In that year, diagnostic science was not the art it is today. Time went by, and the pain grew worse. Treatments included massage, ultraviolet-ray therapy, and pain medication that did little to help. Gradually Mimi lost feeling in her legs. Paralysis began to spread.

Finally, after three weeks of progressive decline, yet another specialist was called to the house and Mimi was rushed to the hospital. The diagnosis was transverse myelitis with epidural abscess. Perhaps with today's knowledge an accurate diagnosis could have been made sooner and the abscess removed before it partially severed her spinal cord. As it was, after two surgeries, a blood transfusion, and several weeks of hospitalization, Mimi had lost the use of her lower body. The medical consensus was that she would not live for more than a year.

My grandmother set about nursing my aunt back to health. In spite of the ordeal and bleak prognosis, with the love and care of family and friends and her own positive outlook, Mimi's body healed. Although her lower body would remain paralyzed, she grew strong and able in other ways, and her spirit never faltered. People who knew her then say she spent months in bed but always had a smile for visitors. In her 80s, Mary Metskas was listed in medical record books as the longest-lived wheelchair-bound patient still enjoying excellent health and physical coordination.

The future is not some place we are going to,
but one we are creating. The paths are not to be found,
but made, and the activity of making them changes
both the maker and the destination.

— John Scharr, *Loyalty in America*

Constructing Meaning

So what is this story about? A wonderful woman, a bad break, the power of love and clear vision? Yes, but what else? Why does my aunt come to mind nearly every day? What does she represent, and how do I live a happier life because of her story?

I never saw Mimi as handicapped, probably because she never saw herself that way. She lived life as if she didn't face any impediments. She learned how to get in and out of her wheelchair on her own, move the chair up and down short flights of stairs, and drive a car well into her 70s (she was one of the first to own a car with hand controls). She created beautiful handwork and had a home-based business for many years sewing costumes for a Chicago theater company.

There are days when I'm inclined to feel sorry for myself (I know, stop the presses). I become anxious about a challenge or troubled by conflict, work, or illness. And I see Mimi and the grace she displayed in meeting challenges I can only imagine. In the face of one of life's ultimate "bad breaks," she was a warrior. I know she didn't think of herself that way. I don't imagine she saw herself as anything out of the ordinary. Yet everyone who knew her says the same thing: she was an extraordinary human being. Why didn't she give up at 13? How did she continue to get up every morning and smile at life?

Mimi lived a life of discovery and courage. She took risks, transformed obstacles into opportunities, and did it all with a sense of perspective about her condition that taught me more than all of her loving words and caring acts. As she so often told me, "Judy, life is what you make it." Without fanfare or stress, without knowing that she was even doing anything special, she lived these words every day.

Mimi died at 83, with her sister by her side and her positive outlook intact, still in discovery.

It is impossible to predict what each new day will offer. We do, however, make choices in how we receive each offering—as a burden or a gift. Mimi taught me to discover the gift, and for that I am very grateful.

✳

PRACTICE

Who is your Mimi?

What models do you have who encourage you to live more courageously?

What do they represent, and how do you live differently because of them?

Life Is Just a Bowl of Cherries.
Don't take it serious, life's too mysterious.
You work, you save, you worry so,
But you can't take your dough when you go, go, go,

So keep repeating it's the berries,
The strongest oak must fall.
The sweet things in life, to you were just loaned,
So how can you lose what you've never owned?
Life is just a bowl of cherries,
So live and laugh at it all.

– Lew Brown and Ray Henderson, *Life Is Just a Bowl of Cherries*

Discovery on an Icy Bridge

[T]he impossible challenges of life are the best teachers.

– Amy Mindell, *Metaskills*

Driving home late one night during the first snow of the season, I hit a patch of ice on a slippery bridge and struck the barrier that separates the bridge from the air and the water. I careened off one side of the bridge, slid across three lanes of Interstate 95, and scraped along the barrier on the opposite side. Luckily there weren't any other cars nearby.

As I slid on the frozen surface, my first awareness was fear. Then, as the car connected with the barrier, I was jolted into a powerfully present state of being. What flashed through my mind was: *I don't know what's going to happen, but I'm going to be here for it.* Then, deep calm, peace, and presence.

The car's forward momentum played itself out as I hung tight, watching, waiting, and thoughtless for what was probably a few seconds but seemed much longer. Then a second forceful awareness: *I am not in control. And it's fine.* Although it may seem a contradiction, this was an amazing and wonderful moment that remains with me and continues to teach. I still savor that instant of "not knowing," and the weightlessness of not being in charge. The timelessness of total presence took my breath away.

There are moments when I sense that something
else is going on, something I knew a long time ago,
as though there were once a time when
I knew what was behind all of this
but now I have forgotten.

– Hugh Prather, *Love and Courage*

The sliding eventually stopped. I was miraculously alive and, as far as I could tell, in one piece. The car had come to rest with wheels and underbelly up against the right side of the bridge. The bottom edge of my door was wedged against the roadway, and I saw and smelled smoke. I was still calm. I heard the radio and thought maybe the window controls worked, and they did. As I rolled down my window and looked out, standing before me was a kind and gentle man, whose name I never got, offering me his hand, asking if I was okay, and helping me out to safety. Yes.

State troopers arrived, my guardian left, and I began the path of coming back to the reality of a totaled car and finding my way home on a snowy evening.

Discovery

It took me many months to fully understand what happened that night and to make sense out of those brief moments of heightened perception and power. *What was this place I had inhabited for such a short but meaningful time? How did I get there? Can I find it again?*

In *The Magic of Conflict,* Thomas Crum describes a magical domain that "allows us to move beyond the fight, beyond success, to an open realm of possibility," which he calls *discovery.* By any other name, it would have smelled as sweet that snowy, cold night, when I was able to fully appreciate its essence.

Although I had been in this magical realm before, previous circumstances had not thrust me into it so completely. I had never experienced to this degree how little I know and how not in control I am. With the sideways slide, the crash, and the loss of control, I lost *me* for a moment—my sense of past and future, and the unconscious assumptions I make about the way things are. Although that night I slid into discovery by accident, I decided later that I wanted to go there on purpose and more often.

———•••———

Whatever the present moment contains,
accept it as if you had chosen it.
Always work with it, not against it.

– Eckhart Tolle, *The Power of Now*

———•••———

Choosing Discovery

One of the best places to practice discovery is in conflict— when you think you are right about something but are opposed by someone else's idea of right. To choose discovery in that moment is to intentionally put yourself in the land of not-knowing, to be interested in someone else's story, to let go of the need to control the outcome, and to give yourself the gift and power of seeing the world through other eyes.

In dialogue, instead of arguing and making assertions, you ask your conflict partner questions to which you do not know the answers, and invite her to talk about and clarify her position. Rather than excluding options, you seek to expand them. In discovery, you and your partners in the conflict become explorers, searching for and creating meaning together, problem-solving, and seeking the best solution for all. You understand that you can win only if all win.

When you enter relationship from discovery, you remember that you know nothing about other people (even if you think you do) and you seek to uncover their truth as they see it. As if entertaining visitors from another planet, you inquire how things look to them from their cultural perspective. You don't try to convince them of anything, even when you see the world differently. You realize that the world is so huge compared with your understanding of it, that you might easily have different stories about what is out there.

You may, of course, reveal the landscape on your planet so that others can better appreciate where you live. However, from your space of learning and inquiry, you know deep in your bones that others may never be able to see your view. You give up trying to make that happen and become interested instead. Suddenly, people you have known your entire life appear brand new, old situations are altered, and life is more fun..

***When you change the way you look at things,
the things you look at change.***

— Wayne Dyer, *The Power of Intention*

Daily Practice

The realm of discovery is available everywhere—you needn't wait for an icy bridge. Confronted by the unexpected or unwelcome, you become fascinated with the moment and accept it as if you had chosen it. You decide to suspend judgment and open your mind to what is.

In the middle of a contentious meeting, when you hear yourself blaming co-workers for a problem, shift into discovery instead and ask, "What is it about this issue that's important to each of us?"

The next time you arrive home and find your loved one upset, notice if your first reaction is to put up walls of justification or anger. Instead, minimize defensiveness and ask yourself what you might learn. Say to your partner, "Honey, you seem upset. Anything I can do to help?" You may find that the problem has nothing to do with you. And if it does, you've opened the conversation in a useful way.

Life Happens

When life happens suddenly and unexpectedly in ways that throw you off balance, discovery invites you to be fascinated, curious, and interested. Instead of spending energy in resistance, you find your equilibrium through acceptance and acknowledgement. You watch, listen, feel, and learn. The event becomes your teacher as you find your way through new, unimagined territory that you would otherwise never have known.

We all experience moments of discovery when we break through to a new understanding of our world. Sometimes the breakthrough happens by accident. Our ongoing challenge is to choose to go there on purpose. Thomas Edison's famous words after many attempts at inventing the lightbulb show a man in discovery mode: "I have not failed. I have only found 10,000 ways that won't work!" Katharine Hepburn, who lived a life of stardom but never lost her childlike fascination with people and life, has been quoted as saying, "Wouldn't it be great if people could get to live suddenly as often as they die suddenly?" Shifting to discovery is one way. Try it. Discover for yourself.

※
PRACTICE

Do you know someone who shifts into
discovery when the chips are down?
How does he do it?

Notice how you feel when you
are with people who become curious
and interested when faced with adversity.
Then notice how it feels to be around
someone who shifts into blame or
justification. Who would you rather
be around, and why?

Describe below one situation or
relationship in which you want to
practice being more discovering,
curious, and interested.

_____

_____

_____

_____

_____

_____

_____

_____

_____

MIKE'S STORY

When faced with the prospect of meeting with a confrontational employee, I heaved a sigh. "Not again," I thought. "Every conversation with this guy is a struggle."

Mostly because I had tried just about everything else, I decided to use the meeting as an opportunity to practice discovery and to see how long I could actually stay there with this person. I took a few deep breaths and centered myself.

The employee began by stating with intensity all that was going wrong with our project. My initial reaction was to immediately respond with what should be done and to correct him. I caught myself, re-centered, and sat quietly listening for a while, practicing being curious and open-minded. Instead of coming back with answers or a rebuttal, I found myself asking the employee what he thought the real nature of the problem was and how I could help him solve it.

Befuddled at first, the employee nonetheless seized the moment to deliver his plan, and his thoughts flowed with clarity and energy. The confrontational atmosphere diffused and gave way to a sense of collaboration. My shift in attitude opened the way for some fresh ideas on both sides, and we began to work on solving the issues confronting the project.

Many Lessons

Water is everywhere around you,
but you see only the barriers that keep you from water.

– Rumi

There's a saying in aikido: "There are many lessons on the mat." It means that when we're practicing aikido, we're not just learning aikido, we're also learning about life. For example, when my aikido partner grabs my wrist too hard and I get angry but don't say anything, I eventually learn that it would be more useful to ask him not to grab so hard. I may also notice that it is difficult for me to ask for what I want in other places in my life, that I suffer needlessly because of it, and that I blame others and justify my blaming instead of taking action. Many lessons ...

Swimming Lessons

I swim daily and notice that I have a new saying, similar to the aikido one: "There are many lessons in the pool." Every day, I seem to have another learning adventure.

An example of this is finding a compatible lane partner. Some swimmers are easy and quiet as they cut through the water; others splash. Some swim straight and stay in their own part of the lane, leaving plenty of room. Others flail and lunge, seemingly unaware that there is anyone else around. As in aikido, with some partners cooperation is easy. As if we were dancing, we know the timing and the moves and we flow easily with each other. With others it's messy, and we're stepping on each other's toes all the time. Ever feel this way? At the pool, as in aikido, I find I can make the situation messier or easier depending on my attitude and actions.

Lesson 1: I am given many dance partners in life. Whether the dance is easy or difficult is influenced at least in part by me.

Please Pick Another Lane

Which brings me to Lesson 2. One of the "difficult partners" seems to like to swim with me. I can't figure it out. Even when there's an empty lane, he gets in mine. He swims more slowly than I do, so I have to wait for him or double back so as not to "pass" him, which we're not allowed to do at our pool. He splashes and his swimming is erratic, his arms swinging way out to the side and occasionally accidentally hitting me. When I see him coming, I think, *Oh no, please pick another lane.* But he doesn't.

One morning, I came to the pool late and this gentleman was already swimming. I was sitting on the edge of an open lane next to his doing my warm-ups when he came up for air. He looked over and motioned to me that he was getting out and I could have his lane. I thanked him but stayed where I was. I had a lane. He explained that he really liked his lane because there weren't any jets gushing water into the pool. The jets are very strong and bother him. The lane he was in—the lane I usually swim in—doesn't have them. *Aha!* I say to myself. *He doesn't get into my lane just to annoy me. He dislikes the other lanes. And now he's trying to give me the "good" lane. What a nice person!*

Lesson 2: It's not always about me.

The Benefit of the Doubt

A third lesson from the pool is that people surprise me if I let them. Recently I got into the hot tub ("many lessons in the hot tub") to relax after my swim. There was a man in there swishing his legs back and forth really hard, churning the water into waves. I closed my eyes, leaned against the edge of the tub, and tried to mellow out. Impossible. I opened my eyes and looked at him, hoping he would see that he was disturbing me, but he was oblivious. I closed my eyes again. It was getting worse. I was practically drowning in the churning hot water. I opened my eyes and looked again. He was either unaware or ignoring me. I sighed out loud. No reaction.

Okay, time to either get out of the tub or say something. I remembered that curiosity usually works better than accusation, and I asked, "Is that an exercise you're doing?" He noticed me and smiled—a really nice smile—and said yes, it was an exercise recommended by his doctor. He used to jog, loved jogging, but his knees could no longer support that activity. In fact, his knees could barely support walking, and swimming was one of the few things that helped. The swooshing motion strengthened the ligaments. He went on to talk about jogging, swimming, disappointment and his efforts to reinvigorate his knees and stay in shape. *What a nice man,* I thought.

> Lesson 3: People usually have a positive intention. Give them the benefit of the doubt.

The benefit of the doubt: what does that mean? What doubt? Well, as I swim up and back and up and back, I think it must mean giving other people the benefit that derives from my doubting my preconceived notions about their motives. *Is he really getting in my lane just to annoy me?* Probably not. *Is he churning up the water to keep others out?* I think I'll doubt that assumption and see what happens.

Usually what happens is that I discover a genuinely nice person behind the fog of my assumptions and have a really fun swim.

[I]f you want to change the way you feel about people, you have to change the way you treat them.

– Anne Lamott, *Plan B*

PRACTICE

What situation or relationship could benefit from your giving someone the benefit of the doubt?

Are you making assumptions about someone's actions when it might be more advantageous to check whether your assumptions are accurate?

Moving into discovery means to shift from blame to curiosity. Where can you experiment?

JOE'S STORY

I have been thinking about discovery. In the past, when I would lose a tool or not be able to find something, I would become very stressed out. But for the past few months, whenever I start to search for the misplaced item, I am always thinking to myself, What am I going to find today that I am not even looking for? *Sooner or later, I find most everything I lose, but the sense of discovery is pretty cool.*

5

Power

There is power in this process of alignment,

connection, and discovery.

As I align and connect with the

opposing energy, I gain insight

into the origin of the attack.

By honoring the opponent,

I allow him the freedom to change.

I influence the problem by altering

my relationship to it.

I gain power by changing myself.

*Our deepest fear is not
that we are inadequate.
Our deepest fear is that we are
powerful beyond measure.*

— Marianne Williamson, *A Return to Love*

Beacon Street

Seeing me before him,
The enemy attacks,
But by that time
I am already standing
Safely behind him.

– Morihei Ueshiba, *O Sensei,* Founder of Aikido

I was walking down Beacon Street in Boston one summer day, when a well-dressed, middle aged man approached and asked me for directions to Quincy Market.

It was the middle of the day and, while no one was in the immediate vicinity, there were people around. I kept walking past the place where I imagined that he wanted me to stop. Then I turned to face him and pointed with an expansive gesture in the direction of the market. My voice was loud, clear, and steady as I told him he could probably walk there. I suggested that he go across the street to Starbucks, where he could get more detailed directions.

The interchange lasted no more than ten seconds, but it was full of a subliminal awareness that I was on guard, my senses heightened, my physical ability ready for ... *what?*

Afterward, I remarked on how my body kept moving away from the corner where the initial encounter took place, standing as I was with my back against the fence of the Public Garden. I was pleasantly surprised at how I had created a safe distance between the man and me, giving me freedom to move in any direction.

Once the moment was over, I thought about how big my arm movements had been as I pointed toward the market. I felt larger than my usual self, although not defensive or fearful. I was engaged and fully present, receptive, and assuming good intention on the part of the questioner, although I was ready for any contingency.

It all happened very quickly, and I did not make these instantaneous assessments consciously. Only after I turned the corner onto Charles Street did I begin to reflect on exactly how much had happened in that brief encounter, and its implications about power and influence.

For example, although I had no outwardly perceptible reason to think the man had anything but harmless intentions, my physical response was to keep moving to a safer place on the sidewalk. Maybe it was because I saw another man with his back to us opening the door to a van parked nearby. Or it could have been the sound of the man's voice, the way he inclined his body toward me as he spoke—a bit too close for comfort—or the frightening stories I've read about men, vans, and unsuspecting victims. There's no way of knowing if the man's motives were suspect. I only know that I was able to give him the benefit of the doubt without compromising myself.

Your spirit is the true shield.

– Morihei Ueshiba, *O Sensei,* Founder of Aikido

Appropriate Response

One of the reasons I practice aikido is to train my body and mind to respond appropriately and automatically to the circumstances at hand. In physical danger, I may not have time to think about what to do. My hope is that over time I am creating a kind of internal personal barometer— call it intuition—that will tell me the extent of the danger and what to do about it. So, as I looked back on the Beacon Street interaction, I was pleased. My barometer was working. I had automatically and appropriately kept myself safe while extending positive energy.

As I thought about my response to this encounter, I began to draw parallels to other situations. Which of my "street smarts" might I use in the office, over dinner, or at the conference table? Many conflicts that are not physically threatening may nonetheless evoke a similar effect: my adrenaline begins to pulse, my senses grow more acute, and I react. How might I train for this kind of situation— how can I communicate receptivity *and* confidence, give my partner the benefit of the doubt *and* protect myself?

Ten Seconds

It's interesting how much can happen in ten seconds. My lesson from Beacon Street is that acceptance and preparedness can go hand in hand. While I accept my partner at face value, I am prepared for any change in direction he might take. If he is simply looking for information—or if he means harm—I am prepared. My partner knows this, too.

As I train in physical and verbal aikido, I expand my ability to be open and assertive at the same time. The more I explore these attitudes, the more I'm sure they are not mutually exclusive, but one requires the other.

I need to feel self-assured before I can accept, understand, or appreciate another's position. Likewise, the more I accept my own power, the more I can use it consciously to understand and accommodate.

Purposeful power allows us to be safe and receptive, strong and soft, assertive and approachable at the same time—to say no *and* yes.

———

If your heart is large enough to envelop your adversaries,
you can see right through them and avoid their attacks.
And once you envelop them, you will be able to guide them
along a path indicated to you by heaven and earth.

– Morihei Ueshiba, *O Sensei,* Founder of Aikido

———

✳
PRACTICE

- Recall a recent conversation in which you felt the need to either give in or become belligerent and attacking.

- Envision the scenario again. This time explore how it might be possible to extend your energy in such a way that you are open without being passive. Can you assert your view without being aggressive?

- In general, experiment with holding two seemingly opposing energies in your awareness at the same time. For example:

  - Anger and compassion
  - Fear and curiosity
  - Sadness and hope
  - Frustration and understanding
  - Judgment and appreciation

KAREN'S STORY

*Some time ago, one of my associates was very angry about a provision in
our company policy. She asked for a private meeting and began to tell
me what it was that had so upset her. I couldn't hear anything she was
saying because I was resisting her view. Physically, I could feel my body
clenching, and mentally, I was preoccupied with what I was going to say
when it was my turn to speak. Fortunately, I thought of the aikido
metaphor of blending with the energy of the attack. Almost immediately, I
felt my physical tension drain away, and I found myself listening to her for
the first time since she started talking. I began to ask questions to find out
more of what lay behind the outburst. I became curious, wanting to know
as much as I could. The more I listened, the more I felt I was reclaiming
my power.*

*What I heard was that she was concerned about fairness, clarity of
communication, and the reputation of the company. So was I. We were
on the same side. From this common ground of wanting what was best
for all of us, I explained my view of how the company policy supported
that vision and also helped her. I was able to stay open to some positive
changes based on our discussion and, in the end, to reassert my role as a
leader in the company. We solved the problem, and the conflict became
an opportunity to reinforce our ability to handle other challenging
situations.*

Wearing the Hakama: Lessons in Leadership

There is a vitality, a life force, an energy, a quickening, that is translated through you into action.

– Martha Graham, Dancer and Choreographer

A song by Brian Hyland from the 1960s goes:

It was an Itsy Bitsy, Teeny Weeny, Yellow Polka Dot Bikini,
That she wore for the first time today.
An Itsy Bitsy, Teeny Weeny, Yellow Polka Dot Bikini,
So in the water she wanted to stay.

The song is about a young woman wearing a bikini for the first time. She manages to get into the water but is afraid to come out because someone might see her.

I had a similar feeling the first time I wore my *hakama*.

In our school's aikido tradition, those practitioners who have earned a black belt also earn the right to wear an article of clothing called a *hakama*—a pair of very wide black culottes that fall from waist to ankle and are tied on with four long black straps. This attire signifies that those wearing it are entitled to be called "beginners" in the art of aikido. We've shown that we understand the basics of technique and are ready to learn the subtleties of the art.

Reaching this level usually requires a minimum of six to eight years of committed practice. Before donning the *hakama*, we wear a white practice uniform (called a *gi*) and a white belt.

Of course, those wearing the white *gi* look at the *hakama* as a symbol of leadership. They expect the wearer to know what she's doing, to throw hard, and to be able to handle martial power.

Assuming Leadership

When I first put on a *hakama*, I began to think about the bikini song. Up to this point, although I was the founder of my dojo, I wore a *gi* and looked like everyone else. I was nominally the chief instructor, but in reality most of our classes were taught by visiting instructors from nearby sister schools in Massachusetts and Maine. Putting on the *hakama* meant becoming in fact the chief instructor and the leader in ways I was not sure I knew how to handle. I was afraid to come out of the water.

Luckily I had help. It came first from my brother, Mike, a retired Navy captain. He said he appreciated the feelings I must be having wearing my "new getup" in front of people who understood its importance. He was also confident that I would recognize the responsibility and uphold all of the traditions that came with it.

I realized that people would expect more of me now. That was my fear, of course, and Mike helped me to understand that it was also my new responsibility.

Knowing the steps ahead of time is not important;
being willing to engage with the music and move
freely onto the dance floor is what's key.

– Margaret J. Wheatley, *Leadership and the New Science*

Coming Out

I looked around to see how others wore their *hakama* and
how they handled the rank that it implied. I had many good
role models—excellent teachers who, with patience and
persistence, mentored me, helped our students understand
proper etiquette, and supported our dojo.

I began to walk the path of the leader of the dojo. I
realized my students wanted me to do it and that they were
watching to see if I would take up the mantle. I understood
that to hide in the water would be a disservice to them and
to aikido. I found my center, stood straighter, and walked
onto the mat with an expanded vision. This was in fact my
school. Putting on the *hakama,* I accepted leadership in
form and function, and each new challenge offered new
lessons.

I learned that a skilled leader creates a safe structure. In
an aikido dojo, an unsafe environment could mean someone
gets hurt, and one of my primary functions is to protect. This
means supporting students in safe practice and personal
responsibility. It also means making tough calls to keep
people from accidentally injuring each other. When etiquette

105

is breached, I point it out. When technique is sloppy, I notice and correct it. When commitments are not kept, I speak up.

I have become conscious over the years of the subtle process by which my students, co-instructors, and I create the environment of our school. I think that one of the ways a leader uses her power is to encourage vision. She keeps the vision alive by reminding others of shared goals, rules, and culture. Over time, students enroll in the vision and join in protecting and supporting the environment. In our dojo, more advanced students help beginners by teaching them to bow correctly, seeing that they wear a clean *gi,* showing them how to vacuum the mat, and making them feel at home. We all hold the vision, and gradually new leaders emerge.

Rank and Responsibility

In my work with corporate and government groups, I see many wonderful leaders with their own applications of these principles. In healthy workplaces, leaders are not afraid to lead, nor are they afraid to share leadership. With patience and persistence, they praise where appropriate, offer advice, and make difficult decisions. They promote and support the group's vision and help others to lead.

"Power" and "leadership" are not bad words. There are, of course, leaders who abuse power. But, used consciously, power can support, encourage, and invite collaboration and co-creation. Humility, responsibility, and power can go hand in hand.

I'm no longer afraid to come out of the water. Before practice as I tie on my *hakama,* I feel the traditions that created it and see the people who have worn it before me. A *hakama* covers much more than a bikini, after all. It's warm and made of good strong material. It fits me well, holds my body erect, and even makes my aikido better. It's starting to feel well worn, like an old glove that was initially stiff and unyielding but now slides on easily and feels comfortable. I'm learning to love it and embrace all that it represents.

✳

PRACTICE

In what ways or places are you being
asked to take leadership?
Are you resisting the role or flowing into it?

Sometimes leadership requires us to
be more assertive than we're ready to be.
Other situations call for a quieter guidance, so that
other members of the team can grow.
Can you find examples of each in your "dojo"?

In what circumstances, if any, are you
"afraid to come out of the water"?
What would help you to become the
leader you want to be?

MARIA'S STORY

Whenever I think about leadership, I think about being comfortable in my own skin, and how we, as individuals, are all leaders in some fashion. Confidence—is that what I am talking about? It is important to "wear yourself" with conviction.

What Is This Thing Called Ki?

The spirit that moves an atom, waves the sea, and lifts the flames of a fire is also circulating in each human being.

– Morihei Ueshiba, *O Sensei,* Founder of Aikido

Walking through the main terminal of the Denver International Airport, I was momentarily stopped by a mass of swarming travelers, and I decided to experiment with expanding my *ki*. I envisioned myself surrounded by a large sphere of energy that moved along with me. As I moved into the crowded space, I let my *ki* sphere lead the way. Where there seemed to be no space, gaps suddenly opened in front of me, and I glided effortlessly through them. My *ki* sphere helped me to anticipate a passerby's sudden change of direction, and I easily moved around him and into the space that appeared as if in anticipation. Swimming with the current, I was carried along on an unseen slipstream to my gate.

On the plane, I was seated next to someone about twice my size, who had parked his arm over my armrest, encroaching into my seat space. I felt hemmed in. Hmmm! I expanded my *ki* sphere again, simply imagining it extending beyond me. After a while, my seat partner's arm came down into his lap.

Centered Power

As part of a high school program for peer mediators, twelve students tried an exercise called "The Unbendable Arm." A common teaching tool in the aikido world, "The Unbendable Arm" is a fascinating exploration into the nature of power, into intention, and, ultimately, into the metaphysical realm of just how easy life can be when we shift to a new way of thinking. (You will find a more complete description of the exercise in this story's Practice.)

The high school mediators were great students. Each dutifully put out his arm and held it straight and strong as a partner tried to make it bend at the elbow. Naturally the arm grew tense and rigid, straining under the partner's consistent pressure, each student trying to win the arm-bending contest. Who would be more powerful?

Next the students were asked to try a different kind of power. Keeping the arm relaxed but energized, the students were told to imagine the arm as if it were a fire hose filled with flowing water. The water represents energy that is directed toward something important—a goal, a loved one, a purpose, or a vision. With the focus moved off the arm and onto a larger objective, and with the arm relaxed and filled with energy, the students found they had more power. Not only could a partner not bend the arm, but no effort or strain was required to keep it extended. They were experiencing the power of *ki*.

At the end of the exercise, I asked them to consider what had just happened with questions like: What is power? Who has power over you? What power do you have over yourself?

One student said: "If you had asked me at the beginning of the workshop who had power over me, I would have given you a list a mile long. But now, I feel like nobody has power over me, but me." Another: "There's something else going on here."

This dramatic shift in perception challenges a mental model that equates power with rigid control, inflexibility, and maximum effort. "The Unbendable Arm" demonstrates that inflexibility results in loss of control and that power and effort are not the same. The students felt this in their arms and were catapulted into a new awareness that there is "something else going on here." They began to glimpse a different kind of control by tapping the power of their own unique life energy—the power of *ki*.

Ki *is the cosmic essence of life.*

– Mitsugi Saotome, *Aikido and the Harmony of Nature*

Ki—*Defined*

I anticipate resistance whenever I talk about *ki*. I imagine audiences thinking, "What's this new age mumbo jumbo?" because I was skeptical at first, too. Then I lead them through "The Unbendable Arm," and I see a room full of true believers.

I think we all know that there is "something else going on here." Otherwise, how do you know that something is "off" when you enter a room? Why is it you feel comfortable in the presence of some people but not others? What tells you that your child is in trouble, when he insists that nothing is wrong? When someone smiles, why are you happy? You may not be able to see it, but you are perceiving *ki*.

The invisible substance that enlivens our bodies, our environment, and our relationships, *ki* is a Japanese word variously interpreted as Energy, Spirit, Intention, Breath, Life Force, and Universal Creative Energy. Its Chinese equivalent is *ch'i*. It is essential to many aspects of Asian culture, including medicine, art, philosophy, and physical training. You can cultivate strong, healthy, and powerful *ki* through deep-breathing techniques and by practicing focused concentration. In aikido, we control the opponent by blending with the intent of their *ki* and redirecting it with ours. As it is described by Morihei Ueshiba, "Aikido is realizing the original power of life, *ki*, by harmonizing with the throbbing rhythms of the universe and the laws of nature."

———·•·———

What this power is, I cannot say.
All I know is that it exists ... and it becomes available
only when you are in that state of mind in
which you know EXACTLY what you want ... and are
fully determined not to quit until you get it.

– Alexander Graham Bell

———·•·———

The best way to understand *ki* is through experience. Most of us know the proverbial story in which a small person lifts the weight of a car in order to save a child's life. This is an example of *ki* power in action. In extraordinary moments of personal accomplishment, when you feel fully present and alive, your *ki* expands. When you feel the strong connection between yourself and another human being, you're feeling the connection of *ki*. If you've ever said, "That was too easy,

I wasn't doing anything," you were experiencing the power of *ki*. We also experience *ki* when we are moved by a great performance in the arts or sports. The flow of graceful movement, the expansive quality of poetry and opera, and the thrill you feel when the home run goes over the fence all represent the unquantifiable sensation of heightened *ki*.

Energy Fields

Conversely, when you are feeling small, fearful, or defensive, your *ki* contracts. You may feel stuck and unable to move forward or make decisions, because your life energy has stopped flowing.

Ki is everywhere—it is the water in which we are swimming through life. Because we can't see it, we tend not to think about it, or we place it in some "new age" category that is easy to dismiss. Yet scientists have shown that unseen energy fields affect our actions, thinking, and relationships. When we walk into a room and sense something, we're sensing the room's energy—*ki*—field. When everyone denies a problem that we all know exists but are reluctant to talk about, the unresolved energy is "hidden *ki*" that stays in the background and influences everything anyway.

What is relevant here is that we can influence the hidden *ki*. When I walk into that room, the energy field created by the people, objects, and feelings that are in it—the *ki* that is already present—may influence me. But I influence it as well. I center and breathe, and my *ki* expands. I feel more confident, capable, and ready to engage. Events follow from that choice. If I hold my breath, become nervous, and contract my *ki,* different events will follow.

Understanding how our choices affect our *ki* is a critical element in recognizing how we collaboratively create our environments and our lives. Although we can't see it, *ki* is the stuff that we, and our relationships, are made of.

———·•·———

Look at this window: it is nothing but a hole in the wall,
but because of it the whole room is full of light.
Being full of light it becomes an influence by
which others are secretly transformed.

— Chuang Tsu, Taoist Teacher and Poet

———·•·———

Giving and Receiving

To have a personal experience of *ki,* find a partner and try "The Unbendable Arm" exercise (see page 115). When you feel the difference in your own mind and body between these two ways of being, you will be able to put the metaphor to work. You'll start to notice that—just like the exercise—expanding your *ki* has a positive effect on you and your environment, all in the space of an instant.

For example, consider a recent argument that did not go well. How would you describe your *ki*—expanded or contracted? Was your body tense? Were you holding your breath? That is contraction of *ki*. Were you breathing, relaxed, and centered? That's expansion or extension of *ki*. Your *ki* influenced the outcome of that situation as much as anything you said (or didn't say).

Regardless of how well you plan your words, if your *ki* is contracted, your partner in the conflict will tend to "catch" your energy and respond in like manner. If you relax and extend *ki,* your partner will correspondingly sense that and have an opening to do the same.

You can gain awareness of and access to your *ki* so that contraction and expansion are not accidental. You can make choices about whether you contract or expand. When giving a presentation or performance, if you are fearful of the audience, your tendency will be to contract and withdraw energy from them. The audience will do the same and withdraw from you. Instead, extend *ki* that includes the audience members by changing your thoughts about them or by physically centering yourself, breathing, and feeling your mind and body open. The audience will respond with a similar expansion and be more receptive to what you have to offer.

Sensitivity to *ki* is a learned awareness, and the ability to direct your *ki* on purpose improves with practice. Aikido teaches that you need not fear your power. When used consciously, the power of *ki* is engaged, aware, and fluid. You learn to move with the strong energies you meet and to influence them in return.

Our high school students knew that they were onto something when they experienced a power that opened new realms of self-control previously unknown to them. What is power? Who has power over *you*? What power do you have over yourself? You might ask yourself the same questions. And watch as you live the answers.

*
PRACTICE

The Unbendable Arm

(Adapted from *The Magic of Conflict,* by Thomas Crum.)

1. With a partner standing by your side, extend your arm in front of you with your thumb up.

2. Have a partner grasp your arm, one hand under your wrist, the other over your bicep.

3. Allow your partner to bend your arm at a right angle to get a feel for the movement and then straighten your arm out again.

4. Now, make a fist and attempt to be so strong that your partner won't be able to bend your arm (no broken bones, please). Notice the amount of energy and effort it takes to keep your arm straight.

5. Next, open your fist and visualize something or someone important to you across the room. Imagine a stream of energy or water flowing from your fingers and your extended arm to the visualized person or thing. Wiggle your fingers as if spraying your energy toward your vision.

6. While you are connecting in this way, have your partner resume trying to bend your arm in a slow fashion.

7. Your arm should bend less than before, with considerably less effort on your part.

DREE'S STORY

After our special needs instructors' group took your course on conflict resolution, several of us used it successfully at a parent meeting. Three or four of us were going into what we anticipated would be a stressful meeting about one of our students.

In preparation, we gave each other the "secret sign" as we passed in the hall—the "The Unbendable Arm." We left little signs on each other's room doors with the reminder "Center" on it. By the time we got into the meeting, it went off without a hitch. The atmosphere was calm and cooperative, and we all left far more relieved than we thought possible.

I think changing the energy in the atmosphere around the situation did the trick before the meeting even started. Even the parents left in good shape! It was mentally embracing the idea that things could go well— rather than draining our energy by anticipating how badly things could turn out—that made the difference.

Inventing Your Life

You have brains in your head.
You have feet in your shoes
You can steer yourself
any direction you choose.

– Dr. Seuss, *Oh, the Places You'll Go!*

In one of my first jobs, an astute teacher taught me to set aside a few minutes every day, close my eyes, and visualize what I wanted in my future—knowledge, confidence, income, relationships, awards. The only limit was my imagination. I decided to dream big and envisioned myself earning an income that, at the time, seemed beyond my reach. After a year of visualizing the goal every day, I achieved it.

While training for my aikido black belt, I complemented intense physical preparation with daily visualization. Each morning I sat quietly, closed my eyes, and imagined the test from beginning to end. In my mind's eye, I saw myself executing each technique clearly and powerfully, with good posture and easy breathing. I imagined my satisfaction at the test's successful completion. When I took the actual test, I felt as though I had been there already, and it unfolded pretty much as I'd envisioned it.

I have employed this visualization technique in many situations and have discovered it to be magical in its ability to manifest the specific images I dream up. When the power of imagination is connected with ability, desire, and knowledge, anything is possible.

Imagination is more important than knowledge.

– Albert Einstein

Imagination and Evolution

Birthing the new out of the old through the power of imagination is not a new concept. Nature provides many examples. In *Earthdance: Living Systems in Evolution,* Elisabet Sahtouris writes about the evolutionary process of the caterpillar, which contains within its biology certain "imaginal disks." The disks are isolated from one another, and as long as they remain in that condition, the caterpillar remains a caterpillar. But when the disks begin to connect, they form "imaginal cells," which eventually combine with other cells to become the butterfly. The remainder of the caterpillar body turns to food for the new being.

The caterpillar's imaginal disks have a built-in, cellular knowledge that gives them direction. Do human beings have similar "imaginal disks"? In each moment of life, we make decisions that move our lives along a certain path. But is that path taking us where we want to go? To paraphrase an ancient Chinese proverb, unless we change our direction, we are likely to end up where we're headed.

I've learned that in order to know where I am headed and eventually get there, two actions are required: I must continue to clarify the destination, and I must move consistently toward it.

I have also learned that I am shaped by my path and by the destination. For example, as I see myself living in my imagined future, I gradually take on the sensibilities of the person I'm becoming. This happens both on the conscious level, as I clarify and reinforce my vision, and on another level that is beyond my conscious thought and action. There is "something" working behind the scenery, something that I have learned to trust.

———

Does this path have a heart? If it does, the path is good; if it doesn't, it is of no use…. One makes you strong; the other weakens you.

— Carlos Castaneda, *Teachings of Don Juan*

———

Be Careful What You Wish For

The more specific I can be about what I want, the better. And I am careful not to waste mental energy on what I don't want. If it's true that what I think about tends to manifest, it's important to imagine a positive future.

Bearing this in mind, I wonder whether efforts at visualization can go beyond the immediate worlds of work and home. As a global community, does the way we think about the future of our planet help to bring that future about? In *Dreaming the Dark,* author Starhawk suggests that, in fact, we "dream the world into being" with our hopes and fears about the future. She cautions us to dream with awareness lest we inadvertently dream up our worst nightmares.

The implications of this notion are awe-inspiring. When we read the morning news, do we contract in fear or open ourselves to possibility? Do we consistently imagine worst-case scenarios, or can we visualize a world where neighbors and countries live in peace with one another? What about our internal dialogues, those relentless conversations that are the undercurrent of our daily activities? Are they hopeful or anxious? Do they weaken or strengthen us? Can they be re-channeled into positive directions to influence our personal, relational, and global connections for the better?

You must become aware that you are dreaming all the time.
Only with awareness do you have the possibility of
transforming your dream.

— Don Miguel Ruiz, *The Four Agreements*

Focused Attention

We live in challenging times. We're under pressure not only in our high-stress work environments but also from the high-conflict/high-drama state of world affairs. This climate affects our minds, bodies, and spirits. Faced with these situations, most of us resort to either fighting back or staying hidden in our cocoons.

But there is a third way: stepping out of the contest to imagine and work toward a different and positive future.

When we purposefully imagine a positive future, we are taking the first steps toward making it a reality. The present moment and the future are intimately connected, one growing out of the other. How we use the present directly affects our future. Conversely, the way we imagine the future affects our actions in this moment.

Caterpillar to Butterfly

Sahtouris points out that as we evolve as human beings on this planet, we must not focus on the sludgy remains of the caterpillar, but on what we're becoming—the butterfly. Prayer, visualization, meditation, imagining, dreaming—these quiet practices help us access our own imaginal disks. As we nourish our visions of ourselves, our work, and the world we want, we give our imaginal disks time to connect and grow into cells.

While visualization may seem mysterious, it's a simple three-step process that can be done by anyone:

1. Sit quietly.

2. Close your eyes.

3. Imagine what you want to achieve.

In her book on the art and practice of centering, *From Chaos to Center,* aikidoist and *qi gong* instructor Judy Warner points out that without vision, it is difficult to be truly powerful. Vision focuses energy, inspires action, and supports us during difficult times. It is the key to a life of purpose, clarity, and connection. And it is within our grasp.

*I like to think of myself as an artist, and my life is my greatest
work of art. Every moment is a moment of creation, and each
moment of creation contains infinite possibilities.*

– Shakti Gawain, *Creative Visualization*

What are you going for in your life? What could we
accomplish if we began to imagine a world of peace and
abundance? How we get there will reveal itself if we hold the
vision and allow it to guide our conversations. We do not yet
know what is possible beyond the realm of the material
world. To experiment takes only thought and intention. We
are creating our world every day. We may as well do it on
purpose.

✳

PRACTICE

Find ten minutes each day to experiment with creative visualization:

1. Sit quietly.

2. Close your eyes.

3. Imagine what you want to achieve.

How would you like your life to unfold? What kind of world do you want to inhabit? Be specific. Use all your senses. See, feel, hear, taste, and smell your future. How will you walk, talk, smile, and be? How do you want to handle fear, uncertainty, and conflict? Where will you be living? Who are you becoming?

Goals can be material, physical, mental, or spiritual. Short or long term. Personal or planetary. Your only limit is your imagination.

Examples

- You have an important presentation coming up this afternoon. See yourself giving it with poise, equanimity, clarity, and power. See the outcome you want. Hear the praise and feel satisfaction with a job well done.

- Is your life out of balance? Close your eyes and visualize the balanced life that eludes you at present and how you will feel when you have it. The more sensory details you can add, the closer you'll come to receiving what you ask for.

Last night, as I was sleeping,
I dreamt—marvellous error! –
that a spring was breaking
out in my heart.
I said: Along which secret aqueduct,
Oh water, are you coming to me,
water of a new life
that I have never drunk?

Last night, as I was sleeping,
I dreamt—marvellous error! –
that I had a beehive
here inside my heart.
And the golden bees
were making white combs
and sweet honey
from my old failures.

Last night, as I was sleeping,
I dreamt—marvellous error! –
that a fiery sun was giving
light inside my heart.
It was fiery because I felt
warmth as from a hearth,
and sun because it gave light
and brought tears to my eyes.

Last night, as I slept,
I dreamt—marvellous error! –
that it was God I had
here inside my heart.

Is my soul asleep?
Have those beehives that labor
at night stopped? And the water
wheel of thought,
is it dry, the cups empty,
wheeling, carrying only shadows?

No, my soul is not asleep.
It is awake, wide awake.
It neither sleeps nor dreams, but watches
its clear eyes open,
far-off things, and listens
at the shores of the great silence.

— *Times Alone, Selected Poems of Antonio Machado,*
translated by Robert Bly

6

Teachers

Teachers are all around me.

They show me what I've been avoiding,

resisting, and ignoring.

Sometimes I don't see them as teachers.

Often they are unwitting in their instruction.

But my newfound insight into resistance

and discovery allows me to

turn even a would-be tormentor

into a helpful life coach.

Everything that happens
to you is your teacher.
The secret is to learn
to sit at the feet
of your own life
and be taught by it.

— Polly B. Berends,
Whole Child, Whole Parent

Where's the Struggle?

*Surrender is ... the conscious
and unconscious dismantling
of how we thought things should be,
to make way for the way things will,
in fact, occur.*

– Daphne Rose Kingma, *Finding True Love*

I was in the middle of presenting two workshops and about
to begin a third when I found out I had pneumonia. There
was no question I had to stay in bed. Just moving from
one room to another exhausted me. At first, I thought I'd
be well fairly quickly, so I delayed workshops and other
appointments for a week. But in a week I was worse, so
I delayed for another week. Still no better.

Pneumonia is a frightening disease. For starters I couldn't
breathe the way I'm used to breathing. The fluid in my lungs
whistled and gurgled with each inhalation, and talking was
an effort. Second, I coughed so hard my ribs ached. My body
and skin hurt as I moved from chills to hot flushes and back
again. In addition to the physical symptoms, I was feeling
depressed, fearful, and guilty for being sick instead of healthy.

Around the end of the second week of illness and misery,
I began to ask my two favorite questions when I get into a
conflict and am feeling stuck:

• What am I resisting?

• What am I supposed to learn here?

In the physical art of aikido, you learn quickly that you cannot make your opponent/partner do anything he doesn't want to do, especially if he's bigger than you. You can't force the technique. Well, I suppose you can, but then it's not aikido.

Your partner *will* attack—that is his job. You can, however, adapt, and herein lies the key to aikido. By arranging my body differently in relationship to my partner, I gain leverage. I get the laws of physics on my side so that size doesn't matter. If I resist or coerce, the struggle intensifies. If, on the other hand, I can figure out where I'm resisting, where the stuck point is, I can join with my partner's movement, free myself, and influence the outcome.

What Am I Resisting?

In the case of my struggle with pneumonia, I saw myself pushing back against my illness. I had made it into a contest that I was clearly not going to win. It took the shape of inner dialogue: *I should be teaching, I'm letting people down. I hate this. I should be well by now. Why does this have to happen to me?* And I continued to put ongoing commitments on hold for a week at a time, instead of facing the reality that the pneumonia could last a lot longer.

The harder I fought, the more frightened, frustrated, and depressed I became. Finally I asked the question, "What am I resisting?" And I thought: *I'm creating this struggle by resisting being sick. What if I move out of the way by accepting that the illness is real, is here, and may last awhile? I'll lie down until I'm well and see what happens. When it's time to get up, I'll know it.*

Problems can teach us to be gracious, humble, and patient.

– Richard Carlson, Ph.D., *Don't Sweat the Small Stuff … And It's All Small Stuff*

What Am I Supposed to Learn Here?

I'm not saying it was easy to stop struggling. Like centering, at first I had to remind myself continually of my new thinking. But I did get well. In fact, the moment I gave up *needing* to be well, I started to feel better. And I learned something else. As I let go of everything that was telling me how I should be, I could just be. My new focus was on taking care of myself, with lots of sleep, rest, good food, and good books. I gave myself permission to stay in bed until I got better. A determined teacher, pneumonia taught me that self-care is an important gift I can give myself at any time. I don't have to wait for an illness to force me to lie down.

This turned out to be a special time in my life, one I remember with fondness, and I learned I could bring much of its beauty back with me into health. Now when I feel tired—and sometimes when I don't—I go back to my "sickbed" and lie there for a moment or two, or ten, or more, and remember the cocoon I crawled into not that long ago. I bring back the quiet, protected state that helps not only when I'm sick, but every day.

There are times, then, when in order to keep ourselves in existence at all we simply have to sit back for a while and do nothing.

– Thomas Merton, Trappist Monk, Poet, and Writer

✳ PRACTICE

Is there a situation in your life where you feel stuck? How is it holding you back and how might you look at it differently? Where is the gift of learning that eludes you at the moment? Write down the situation and ask yourself the two questions:

The situation:

_____

_____

_____

What am I resisting?

_____

_____

_____

What am I supposed to learn here?

_____

_____

_____

SONJA'S STORY

I had to take my husband to the hospital on Friday because he was so sick with pneumonia, and we were both beginning to get scared. The doctors realized this pneumonia was resistant to the first antibiotic they gave him, so they put him on another, which seemed to make a remarkable difference. He was up on Saturday, moving slowly but not in bed. Sunday, he was moving around more, and today he insisted on doing some errands for me. He's really tough to keep quiet once he feels better. He's talking about going back to work on Wednesday, and I'm advising him not to.

I read your pneumonia story to him, and relayed your experience and advice about rest and stillness. He suffers from that Superman complex that so many seem to be afflicted with. Fortunately, he is also a good listener and is recovering well.

Dancing with "Difficult" People

First of all ... if you can learn a simple trick, Scout, you'll get along a lot better with all kinds of folks. You never really understand a person until you consider things from his point of view ... until you climb into his skin and walk around in it.

– Harper Lee, *To Kill a Mockingbird*

The "difficult" people in our lives can be our greatest source of stress and our best teachers. Because they represent something we resist, they invite us to examine that resistance and the emotions surrounding it. If we are willing to expand our perspective slightly, we may discover new parts of ourselves as well.

I met Jean in a workshop at the beginning of my training career. She had been fighting for years with her daughter-in-law. It seemed they were always on opposite sides of any issue, and none of the ways Jean tried to mend fences worked. She loved her grandchildren dearly, but because of this troubled relationship, she seldom got to see them, which made things even worse.

Changing the Dance

One day Jean and her daughter-in-law were having an argument in which both were locked into opposing views, neither willing to give ground. Jean, however, began to recognize the interaction as a kind of dance they did with each other, one they were both familiar with, and she decided she didn't want to do it again in the same way. She stopped talking, took a deep breath, and said: "I notice we are pretty good at finding things to argue about. What I'd really like is to be a better mother-in-law and a better grandmother to your children. Would you help me? What can I do to make our relationship a better one?"

Her daughter-in-law stopped, too. She didn't know how to react, as, unexpectedly, there was no one to fight with. Could she trust this new Jean? What was her next move? The dance had changed.

In order to have a war, the enemy must be kept alive.

– Terry Dobson, *Aikido in Everyday Life*

True Power

Although it took courage for Jean to change the dance, it was clear the alternative was not working. She didn't want to stay locked in the struggle any longer. The more she pushed her daughter-in-law, the more resistance she encountered. And there were those grandchildren. She was not going to give up. Jean recognized the only person she could change was herself, so she did.

Jean applied aikido principles. Instead of continuing to push back, she made a small gesture of alignment (literally and figuratively) toward her daughter-in-law's side so that a real discussion could begin. By asking how she could be a better grandmother and mother-in-law, Jean invited her adversary to become a partner in problem solving. In so doing, she acknowledged her daughter-in-law's needs for respect and authority. By asking for help, Jean redirected the argumentative energy and utilized it to build the relationship. She honored her daughter-in-law's position and point of view, and a potentially costly conflict turned into an opportunity for greater understanding on both sides.

When our well-being depends upon the actions of others, we inadvertently give them power over us. As you read this story, can you think of someone with whom your "dance" feels like a struggle? A good rule of thumb:

Whenever you find yourself wishing somebody else would change, start with yourself.

This does not mean you're wrong, at fault, or need to change your opinion. It means that if you want to begin to resolve the conflict, it's useful to start with what you can control—yourself. With awareness and practice, you will learn to respond in ways that are more purposeful. By regaining power over yourself, you gain power over the situation.

Jean and her daughter-in-law found more opportunities to dance with conflict as their relationship evolved. Thanks to Jean's willingness to risk, they discovered they had common ground from which to begin the process.

What if your dance partners are not open to new choreography? What if they insist on maintaining an adversarial stance? As long as you are committed to learning, they will continue to be your teacher. And you will discover whether and how you want to be in relationship with them.

We will have challenging people in our lives. Will they be tormentors or teachers? Our perspective greatly influences our response.

———•—

Kurt Vonnegut talks about "wrang-wrangs" in our lives,
great teachers who are placed in our path.
The lessons they teach us are vastly important, and they are
taught through struggle, pain, trial, and tribulation.
Still, they are important teachers.

The next time a "wrang-wrang" drops into my life,
I have the option of recognizing that person as a teacher.

— Anne Wilson Schaef, *Meditations for Women Who Do Too Much*

———•—

PRACTICE

It's hard to like everyone. That seems pretty true in my experience, at least. Some of our colleagues or family members are great partners for us. We know their style and blend easily with their energy. In other words, we "dance well together." With others, we always seem out of step.

Consider that by beginning to understand your opponent, you might turn him or her into a partner, at least for the time you are together. By doing so, you might improve the quality of your life, and who knows, in time you may even become allies.

When a "difficult" person is placed in your path, try something different:

- **See the person as an opportunity to improve your practice of centering.**

- **Experience people as they are, not as you judge them to be.** There is a difference.

- **Imagine what their positive intention is.** What are their hopes? What are they really going for?

- **Be aware of your tendency to react.** Just notice it.

- **Meet the person on "neutral ground."** Find a common interest. Ask about a topic that he or she loves to talk about.

- **Shift your perspective.** Pretend this person is someone you don't know but admire. Imagine he or she is from a different culture or time period. Listen for something new.

- **See a new part of this person.** Notice the caring grandmother, capable colleague, or doting father. Find something to appreciate, in spite of your inclination otherwise.

- **Remember why you are experimenting.** You're stuck and you want to get unstuck. What you've been doing is not working, so try something else.

LINDA'S STORY

I wanted to share with you my interesting Tuesday afternoon. Things starting going awry at approximately 11:00, just after our workshop with you ended. Several of our patients and at least two incoming phone callers were extremely difficult to work with. They were angry, belligerent, and verbally offensive. They wanted to see the doctor, and they wanted to see her now!

I think we were all calm, centered, and, therefore, effective with the patients. When we could not give them what they wanted, we consciously tried not to take their upset attitudes personally. My assistant and I worked together to calm an angry older gentleman, and— most of the time—we were able to come to some mutual understanding with the other patients, without giving offense.

A patient observing from the reception area came to the window and told us we had handled a very difficult patient with dignity and professionalism.

We laughingly wondered later if you had set this all up as our final exam! We definitely had the opportunity to put our lessons to the test.

Unlikely Teachers

*We encourage others to change
only if we honor who they are now.*

– Margaret J. Wheatley and Myron Kellner-Rogers, *A Simpler Way*

Ten-year-old boys can call out the best and the worst in me. One memorable autumn, I had the opportunity to work with fifteen fourth-graders and their parents in a program for "youth at risk." We had been meeting twice a month to talk about conflict and communication within families. This particular night, the boys, their parents, and a toddler whose mom couldn't find a sitter surrounded me. The boys were more than usually active, noisy, and eager for attention. The toddler was not being held in check very well, and there was a general feeling of scattered energy.

At an earlier session, I introduced them to my centering bell, and from that moment, *the bell* became an object of fascination. A small gong made of specially tempered metal, the bell radiates a lovely sound that has the effect of calming and focusing the attention. With each session there had been an increasing clamor about it—when will I ring it, could I ring it now, can they ring it, can they ring it again? Well, this night everyone wanted to ring the bell and everyone wanted to be the *first* to ring the bell. Things were getting a little frantic, and I felt myself resisting their constant requests. So I decided to practice aikido and blend instead.

I had everyone sit down at a round table and told them they would each get a turn to ring the bell. I explained that there were two rules. The first was that each person had to be centered when ringing the bell, and the other was that the whole group had to listen silently until the bell finished ringing—about ten seconds for each ring. I also had one request—that they have clean hands—and proceeded to tell them a story about how I received the bell from my teacher, the power it held, and why it was important they treat it respectfully.

What started out as a way to calm them and satisfy their need to ring the bell ended up being something quite different. Each child (although I hadn't asked) showed me his clean hands (parents, too) as I gave him the bell. He rang it and passed it back to me, and I brought it to the next person. Each time the bell rang, we all listened and centered. By the time it reached the last person, the whole room was centered, quiet, and alive with energy. It was an amazing moment, and all of us knew it.

We must be the change we wish to see in the world.

– Mahatma Gandhi

Centered Teaching

The most important lesson we teach our children is the lesson of "being." Who we are as teachers and how we handle our own conflicts say much more about what we are teaching than the content. It is important to teach the skill—it is more important to live it.

Working with children gives me countless opportunities to learn, discover, and change. They challenge me to model the teaching and ask me to keep my purpose in view. Some of the children I work with don't have many centered role models in their lives. Most do not have a clue about what the word "center" means, but they know it when they see it and feel it.

I lose my center continually with kids. Often, their one job in life seems to be to embody resistance. I start to get angry, resentful, or just plain tired, and then I remember why I'm there. I believe that even if these kids never again practice centering in exactly the way I teach it, they will remember the connection we experienced and an adult who did not see them as an opponent, even when they tried their hardest to be one.

They teach me—by challenging me to blend when I want to resist, daring my center to guide me through what feels like a minefield, each child waiting to see: "Can she practice what she teaches?" And I find the gift of wonder. As I start to balk at their relentless energy, their wanting to go one way when I'm asking them to go another, I remember *O Sensei's* words—"Opponents confront us continually, but actually there is no opponent there"—and I flow into some other world that I never planned to visit but is just the place I want to be.

There are no contests in the Art of Peace. A true warrior is invincible because he or she contests with nothing. Defeat means to defeat the mind of contention that we harbor within.

– Morihei Ueshiba, *O Sensei,* Founder of Aikido

PRACTICE

Think of one person or set of circumstances
that regularly throws you off center.

How will you remind yourself to center
before going into the situation?

How will you remember to re-center periodically?

MARCIA'S STORY

Three first-grade boys came to my office with their teacher to report being bullied by a fourth-grade boy. The fourth-grader had been in the office before for causing similar problems, and he had always denied any wrongdoing, argued with his accusers, and refused to admit responsibility. Consequences such as loss of recess and being made to write apologies had made no impact.

I explained to the three first-graders that they would have an opportunity to talk to the fourth-grader about how his actions had affected them, and although they were nervous about "what they should say," each decided to speak when the fourth-grade "bully" arrived.

Even though his hands were shaking, the first boy to speak addressed the bully by name and said firmly: "I didn't like it when you took our ball and threw it. I didn't like it when you pushed me against the wall. We're just little kids, and you're a big kid. We don't want you to do that to us." Each boy took a turn and spoke about his feelings. I was struck by the impact the boys' words had on the previously unrepentant fourth-grader. He listened quietly to everything they said, and when they finished, he said honestly and without prompting, "I'm sorry."

Thank You Very Much

Very little grows
on jagged rock.
Be ground.

Be crumbled,
so wildflowers will come up
where you are.

You've been stony for too many years.
Try something different.
Surrender.

– Rumi

At Portsmouth Aikido our motto is, "When in doubt, bow!" It's funny—and true. We bow as we enter the dojo. We bow as we get onto the mat. We bow to the teacher as class begins. During class, if a teacher gives individual instruction, we bow to the teacher and then again to our partner. At the end of the class, we bow to each of our partners and offer thanks, using the name of the person we're thanking, as in, "Thank you very much, Kathy." We bow as we get off the mat and bow again as we leave the dojo. These practices are familiar in most dojos across the country and the world.

Choosing Your Attitude

Over the years, I've had many opportunities to thank my fellow students and teachers, and when I say "thank you," I try to mean it. Sometimes that's easy. Some partners are a joy to work with, and it's easy to be sincere. You feel a connection with them that enhances your own energy and feeling of well-being. These partners give energy, and you receive it—then you give and they receive. Power transfers back and forth in an effortless flow. This back-and-forth with a partner feels great and is what aikido is all about.

But it doesn't always happen.

Sometimes I end up practicing with a partner who throws too hard, or one who wants to give instruction when all I want to do is practice, or a beginner who needs instruction when I came to class wanting to practice hard and fast. Still, at the end of practicing with each, I bow and say, "Thank you very much."

Be what you would wish to seem.

– Plato

At first I didn't always feel that my thanks were genuine, but I'd go through the motions anyway. As time went on and I continued in my practice, I began to look for something to appreciate about practicing with *each* person, so that when I said, "Thank you very much," I meant it.

And so it is that my "less than ideal" partners become my teachers. With the partner who throws too hard, I learn how to take care of myself because I have to stay present and use proper technique to fall safely. With the "instructor-partner," I learn patience, appreciation, and maybe even a thing or two I didn't know about the technique. With a partner who is a beginner, I learn through teaching, and I learn patience once again. At the end of class, as I bow to these partners and say, "Thank you very much," I know that my thanks are real. I may not get to choose my partner, but I can choose my attitude.

Life Lessons

From my first aikido teacher I learned the saying, "There are many lessons on the mat," and it has been quite wonderful to learn this one. Equally wonderful is noticing that I can take my "thank you very much" mind-set off the mat.

This mind-set supports me in workshops with challenging students when, instead of trying to prove I'm right, I choose to be grateful for the opportunity to see whether what I'm teaching really does apply to the student's situation. I bow (internally) and think, *Thank you very much.*

I find this thinking also comes in handy as I rush up to the checkout line only to find there's a person ahead of me who needs a price check or can't find his wallet, and my momentum comes to a halt. I think, *Thank you very much,* and look for something to be grateful for—like a chance to breathe and be aware of living this moment of my life.

The difficulty can be anything or anyone who feels like a conflict. I bow to it, say, "Thank you very much," and wait for the gift.

You take the action, and the insight follows.

– Anne Lamott, *Plan B*

The end of the story (or perhaps the beginning) is that this sense of appreciation is growing. I say "thank you" more often, and I increasingly see what there is to be grateful for.

Although simple in principle, the execution of this attitudinal alchemy is complicated. It requires nothing less than changing myself. But as I make progress, my most difficult characters and situations turn out to be my most powerful teachers.

I try to remember now to look for one opportunity every day to practice this technique. Just think—if I can change everything I struggle with into an unexpected gift, what a difference it will make in my life!

It brings new meaning to something author Annie Dillard says: "How we spend our days is, of course, how we spend our lives." And I ask myself, would I rather spend my life in gratitude or frustration?

Crazy question? Maybe, but I'm still practicing, too. As I meet each new partner—and each old one—ah, yes … "Thank you very much."

All meaningful and lasting change begins on the inside.

– Martin Luther

PRACTICE

Play the "Thank-You-Very-Much Game."

- Make a resolution to look for one opportunity every day to practice saying "thank you very much" to a person or situation that you find difficult, annoying, or upsetting. Say it to yourself without necessarily knowing why and see what happens.

- If you like, keep a journal of the situations you choose and the results of your internal shift.

- If you could change everything you struggle with into an unexpected gift, what difference would it make in your daily life?

KATE'S STORY

*The day before my thirty-fifth birthday, I decided to stop at Dunkin'
Donuts on my way to work. On the way out of the parking lot, my red
sports car was hit by a large old van pulling in. My immediate reaction
was to jump out of my car and begin yelling. I shouted, "Don't you have
enough room in your own lane?"—along with a few other choice words—
while the woman in the van was getting out, stammering her apologies,
and trying to explain through my shouting that it was truly an accident.*

*At that moment, my brain registered what I had just learned the day
before in a seminar at work. We were taught to center ourselves before
reacting in anger, and to try and take a different perspective on the
conflict. Normally I would have kept on fighting, insisting on me being
right and her being wrong. Instead I chose to stop, center, and listen to
what the other person was saying.*

*In my anger at my precious car being damaged, I may never have
heard that she was on her way to be with one of her fourteen adopted
children who was undergoing surgery that morning at Children's Hospital
in Boston. Because I did listen, suddenly my repairable car meant very
little, and I met an incredible human being who gives enormously to
others and who touched my life by helping me realize how insignificant
the little things are. If all I remember from those classes is to center, that
alone will change my life and the kind of energy I send out to others daily.*

Afterword

See You on the Mat

If any of these stories have helped you to see your life or work differently, please email judy@judyringer.com and tell me.

Although I've been working with these principles for many years, I still lose my center frequently. My buttons get pushed, I advocate instead of listen, and I take life way too seriously. Every day is a learning experience and an opportunity to "get on the mat." Perhaps that's the point of writing: it's one more way to practice by getting on paper what I believe to be practical ways to make life more artful, effortless, and fun. By writing it down, it becomes more real.

As I teach, I practice centering and extending *ki*, and gradually I become more skilled. Life expands as I flow with the river instead of pushing against it. My center is stronger, and things that used to bother me don't bother me as much. Even when the buttons get pushed, I see it happening sooner and am able to regain my composure more quickly.

A friend and mentor once asked me what I thought my "message" was. Why did I invent this life of teaching and presenting on topics that most people would rather avoid? And the answer is this: The world is getting smaller every day. There are more of us, and more and faster ways to engage. It's easier than ever to step on each other's toes.

We can't continue to allow conflict to get the better of us. We need to wake up to our connection, not only because we might annihilate ourselves if we don't, but also because of the beauty and power of taking down the barriers. We must stop doing the things that don't work and try something else.

I think most of us know this and want to try, but we keep getting in our own way. It's not about countries, or corporations, or special interests. The power to effect change resides in each of us, in every moment, and we have more power than we realize.

Thank you for taking the time to read these stories and for making the space in your own life to, as *O Sensei* said, "practice the art of peace in a vibrant and joyful manner." We're all inventing it as we go along, so let's start doing it on purpose.

Good *ki*!

Judy

You and I are the music,
You and I are the dance
Changing colors, changing partners,
Touching hearts and touching hands.

As we twirl all the world comes alive in our sight
And in the end there is only The Dance.

— Ellen Stapenhorst, *The Dance*

Acknowledgments

***To all my teachers on this writing journey, thank you
for your gifts of time, patience, and loving energy.***

To Thomas Crum, thank you for opening a door that has
led to so many others. The years spent with you as student
and assistant have given me the lens through which I view
aikido. And you are definitely the first person I heard use
the words "conflict" and "opportunity" in the same sentence.
This book is a direct result of our work together and an
expression of my gratitude.

To my fellow trainers and learners on the Aiki Works team,
thank you for your love, support, and unending generosity,
especially Judy Warner's continuous encouragement, timely
suggestions, and kind mentoring; Ellen Stapenhorst's heart and
music; and Glenn Dutton's humor, play, and presence.

Thank you to Janice George, Tom Dubois, Donna Melillo,
and Janet Thompson—my "group"—and to Joy Jacobs and
my processing friends in the World Work community for
listening to my stories over the years and giving me the
courage to write them down, and in whose presence I came
to understand their deeper meaning.

Many thanks to Lisa Noonis, my creative mentor, for
seeing me before I saw myself and for translating that vision
onto paper, for encouraging me with your *oohs* and *aahs,*
and for leading me to the right people at the right time. To
my editor, Sonja Hakala, for understanding what I wanted to
say, helping me to say it, and shepherding me on the journey
of book publication, and to Kara Steere for your careful and
precise copyediting.

Thank you Carol Dudley, Craig Wich, Susan Losapio, Ellen Fineberg, Cindy Harriman, Ann Souto, Ann Driscoll, Sandy Davis, Karen Valencic, Al Delaney, Ron Houle, Fiona Blyth, and Sharon Kanai, for your gentle reading, generous guidance, and loving suggestions that helped shape this book. To my assistant Cindy Morse for the innumerable ways you supported me in this process. And thank you, *Aikido Today Magazine,* for the confidence I gained by seeing my stories in print for the first time.

I owe a debt of gratitude to the late Mitsunari Kanai Sensei and my fellow students and teachers at New England Aikikai, Portland Aikido, and Framingham Aikikai. What I know of the physical art of aikido is due to your patience, encouragement, and constant urging for me to find and use my power. Thank you very much.

Thank you to my students and partners at Portsmouth Aikido, for choosing aikido, embracing me as your teacher, and falling down and getting up again every Tuesday, Thursday, Friday, and Sunday.

To everyone who has participated in my trainings over the years, thank you for your teaching. Although you thought I was the instructor, it was actually the other way around. And my special thanks to those who have shared their own stories, many of them printed in this book.

Thank you, lastly and most importantly, to Mom, Mike, Debbie, Susan, and Paula—for teaching me about conflict and communication by asking me to be a better daughter and sister. And especially to my husband, Jim—lifelong aikido partner, best friend, editor, and muse. This book is as much yours as mine. I love you. Thank you very much.

Permissions

Arnold Mindell, Ph.D.: *The Leader as Martial Artist: An Introduction to Deep Democracy,* HarperCollins, 1992.

Amy Mindell, Ph.D.: *Metaskills,* New Falcon Publications, 1995.

Random House and Dr. Seuss: *Oh, the Places You'll Go!* by Dr. Seuss, TM & copyright © by Dr. Seuss Enterprises L.P. 1990. Used by permission of Random House Children's Books, a division of Random House. Inc.

From the book *The Four Agreements* © 1997, don Miguel Ruiz. Reprinted by permission of Amber-Allen Publishing, Inc. P.O. Box 6657, San Rafael, CA 94903. All rights reserved.

Anne Wilson Schaef, Ph.D.: *Meditations for Women Who Do Too Much*. HarperCollins, 1990.

Margaret J. Wheatley: *Leadership and the New Science,* Berrett-Koehler, © Margaret Wheatley, 2001. Used by permission.

Margaret J. Wheatley and Myron Kellner-Rogers: *A Simpler Way,* Berrett-Koehler, © Margaret Wheatley and Myron Kellner-Rogers, 1996. Used by permission.

The Dance, by Ellen Stapenhorst, © 1987, Pretzel Music. Used by permission. All rights reserved.

"Life Is Just a Bowl of Cherries," ("Composition") by Ray Henderson and Lew Brown © 1931 (renewed) Chappell & Co. and Ray Henderson Music. All Rights Reserved. Used by Permission, Warner Bros. Publications U.S. Inc., Miami. FL 33014.

Resources

The following are some of my favorite books, authors, and Web sites on the topics of conflict, communication, aikido, and inventing your life. I wish you well in your exploration and practice.

For more information and practices on centering, I refer you to the excellent resources of Aiki Works, Inc., which include:

- Thomas Crum. *The Magic of Conflict*. New York: Simon & Schuster, 1987.

- Thomas Crum. *Journey to Center*. New York: Simon & Schuster, 1997.

- Thomas Crum. *Three Deep Breaths*. San Francisco: Berrett-Koehler, 2006.

- Judith S. Warner. *From Chaos to Center*. Aspen, CO: Aiki Works, Inc., 1999.

- The recordings of Ellen Stapenhorst, including *The Dance* (KiNote Productions, 1987); *Invisible Threads* (KiNote Productions, 1994); *All of My Skies* (KiNote Productions, 1998); *Come Back Home* (KiNote Productions, 2004).

Additional reading on conflict, communication, and personal and organizational effectiveness

- Sylvia Boorstein. *It's Easier Than You Think: The Buddhist Way to Happiness*. New York: HarperCollins, 1997.

- Steven Covey. *The 7 Habits of Highly Effective People*. New York: Simon & Schuster, 1989.

- Sandy Davis. *The Recipe for Resilience: Three Simple Practices for Staying Unfrazzled*. Boston: Changewise, Inc., 2005.

- Roger Fisher and William Ury. *Getting to Yes*. New York: Penguin Books, 1991.

- Shakti Gawain. *Creative Visualization.* San Rafael, CA: New World Library, 1978.

- Daniel Goleman. *Emotional Intelligence.* New York: Bantam Books, 1997.

- Andrew LeCompte. *Creating Harmonious Relationships: A Practical Guide to the Power of True Empathy.* Portsmouth, NH: Atlantic Books, 2000.

- Harriet Lerner. *The Dance of Connection.* New York: Harper Collins, 2002.

- Amy Mindell, Ph.D. *Metaskills.* Tempe, AZ: New Falcon Publications, 1995.

- Arnold Mindell, Ph.D. *The Leader as Martial Artist: An Introduction to Deep Democracy.* San Francisco: HarperCollins, 1992.

- Kerry Patterson, Joseph Grenny, Ron McMillan, and Al Switzler. *Crucial Conversations.* New York: McGraw-Hill, 2002.

- Don Miguel Ruiz, M.D. *The Four Agreements.* San Rafael, CA: Amber-Allen Publishing, 1997.

- Anne Wilson Schaef. Ph.D. *Meditations for Women Who Do Too Much.* New York: HarperCollins, 1990.

- Philip Simmons. *Learning to Fall: The Blessings of an Imperfect Life.* New York: Random House, 2002.

- Douglas Stone, Bruce Patton, Sheila Heen. *Difficult Conversations: How to Discuss What Matters Most.* New York: Viking Penguin, 1999.

- Eckhart Tolle. *Power of Now.* Novato, CA: New World Library, 1999.

- Margaret J. Wheatley. *Leadership and the New Science.* San Francisco: Berrett-Koehler, 2001.

- Margaret J. Wheatley and Myron Kellner-Rogers. *A Simpler Way.* San Francisco: Berrett-Koehler, 1996.

- Marianne Williamson. *A Return to Love.* New York: HarperCollins, 1996.

- Rosamund Stone Zander and Benjamin Zander. *The Art of Possibility.* New York: Penguin Books, 2002.

Aikido philosophy, technique, and applications

- David Baum, Ph.D. and Jim Hassinger. *The Randori Principles.* Chicago: Dearborn Trade Publishing, 2002.

- Andy Bryner and Dawna Markova, Ph.D. *An Unused Intelligence.* Berkeley, CA: Conari Press, 1996.

- Terry Dobson. *Aikido in Everyday Life: Giving In to Get Your Way.* Berkeley, CA: North Atlantic Books, 1993.

- Terry Dobson. *It's a Lot Like Dancing: An Aikido Journey.* Berkeley, CA: Frog Ltd., 1994.

- George Leonard. *The Way of Aikido: Life Lessons from an American Sensei.* New York: Penguin Books, 2000.

- Wendy Palmer. *Intuitive Body: Aikido as a Clairsentient Practice.* Berkeley, CA: North Atlantic Books, 1994.

- Wendy Palmer. *The Practice of Freedom: Aikido Principles as a Spiritual Guide.* Berkeley, CA: Rodmell Press, 2002.

- Susan Perry and Ronald Rubin. *Aikido Talks: Conversations with American Aikidoists.* Claremont, CA: Areté Press, 2001.

- Judy Ringer. *Ki Moments* electronic newsletter. Portsmouth, NH: OnePoint Press, 2006.

- Judy Ringer. *Power & Presence* newsletter. Portsmouth, NH: OnePoint Press, 2006.

- John Stevens. *The Philosophy of Aikido* (and other aikido books by John Stevens). New York: Kodansha International, 2001.

- Richard Strozzi-Heckler. *Aikido and the New Warrior.* Berkeley, CA: North Atlantic Books, 1985.

- Alexandria A. Windcaller. *Leading Chaos.* Athol, MA: Haleys, 2002.

Web sites:

The following Web sites offer information, books, videos, exercises, free newsletters, and excellent articles on aikido, difficult conversations, conflict transformation, and self-improvement:

- www.actiondesign.com
- www.aikiworks.com
- www.aikidoonline.com
- www.bodymindandmodem.com
- www.crucialconversations.com
- www.judyringer.com
- www.onepointpress.com
- www.publicconversations.org
- www.resilienceworks.com
- www.triadcgi.com
- www.unlikelyteachersbook.com

About the Author

Judy Ringer is a speaker, author, seminar leader, professional singer, and black belt in aikido. She is founder and chief instructor of Portsmouth Aikido, in Portsmouth, New Hampshire, and sole owner of Power & Presence Training.

As a professional trainer, Judy employs aikido principles to provide unique programs that support a variety of workplace needs. She blends various communication and conflict resolution models with insights gleaned from more than a decade of aikido practice, business ownership, and mind/body training. She lives her belief that we invent our lives moment to moment, and that through practice and conscious intention, we can truly create the life and world we want.

A native of suburban Chicago and graduate of Vassar College, she has lived in Portsmouth with her husband, Jim, since 1974.

For more information on training programs or speaking engagements for your organization, please contact:

Power & Presence Training
76 Park Street
Portsmouth, NH 03801-5031
www.judyringer.com

Order Form for Unlikely Teachers

Email orders: judy@judyringer.com

Web orders: www.UnlikelyTeachersBook.com

Postal Orders: OnePoint Press, 76 Park Street, Portsmouth, NH 03801-5031. USA.

Please send me _____ **copies of** _Unlikely Teachers at $15.00._

Please contact me about: __Speaking/Seminars __CDs/E-book

Name _____

Address _____

City _____ State _____ ZIP _____-_____

Telephone _____

Email _____

Shipping:

United States: _$5.00 for the first book; $2.00 for each additional book._ International: _$12.00 for the first book; $6.00 for each additional book (estimate)._

Payment:

☐ Check

☐ Credit card __Visa __MasterCard __AMEX __Discover

Card number _____

Name on card _____ Exp. date____/____

Ki Moments

Enjoy Judy Ringer's practical suggestions and inspirational reflections each month by receiving her free e-newsletter, _Ki Moments._ Visit www.judyringer.com or subscribe below.

____ **Please subscribe me to your e-newsletter,** _Ki Moments._